IMAGES
of America

FINGER LAKES
MEMORIES

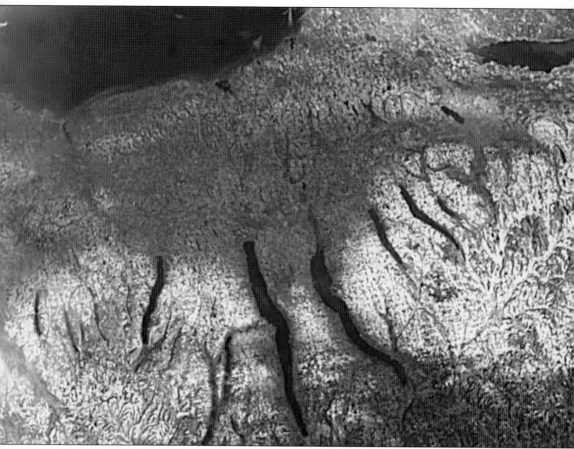

The 11 Finger Lakes are arrayed across New York State like a necklace of slender jewels. At the top of the picture is Lake Ontario. The lakes were formed during the last ice age as a mile-thick sheet of ice began to warm and fracture. The advancing and retreating ice sheets gouged out modern topography. Winter snows accent the lake valleys in this December 4, 2004, photograph taken from the International Space Station. (Courtesy Wikipedia.)

On the cover: Please see page 115. (Courtesy Catharine Corby Gardner.)

IMAGES
of America

FINGER LAKES
MEMORIES

Michael Leavy

ARCADIA
PUBLISHING

Copyright © 2007 by Michael Leavy
ISBN 978-0-7385-4991-0

Published by Arcadia Publishing
Charleston SC, Chicago IL, Portsmouth NH, San Francisco CA

Printed in the United States of America

Library of Congress Catalog Card Number: 2006939087

For all general information contact Arcadia Publishing at:
Telephone 843-853-2070
Fax 843-853-0044
E-mail sales@arcadiapublishing.com
For customer service and orders:
Toll-Free 1-888-313-2665

Visit us on the Internet at www.arcadiapublishing.com

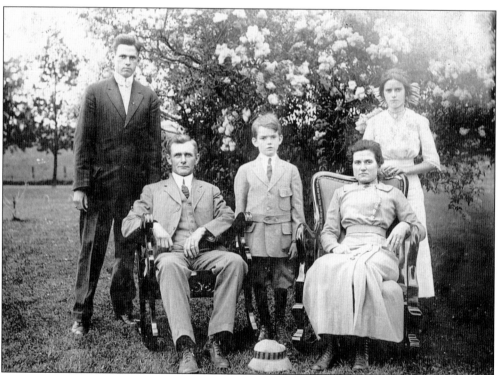

This book is dedicated to my wife, Sandra, and daughters, Rachel and Rebecca. In the image, the Corby family poses on the grounds of their dairy farm, Meadow Brook, in Lima, New York, one of the finest farms in the county. Pictured from left to right are George (standing); his father Oscar, seated; brother Albert (Bruce); then mother, Estella; and daughter Marian (standing). It is dated May 1913, and the lilacs are in bloom.

CONTENTS

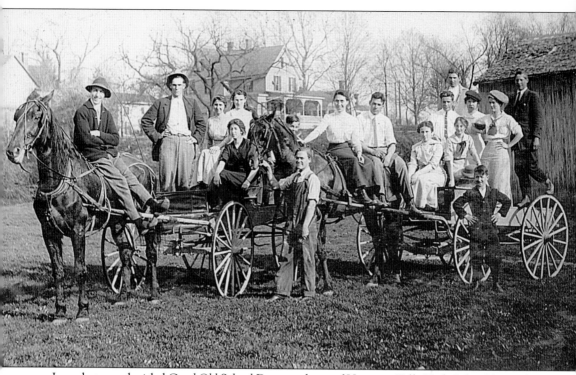

In a photograph titled *Good Old School Days*, students of Honeoye Falls High School have their class picture taken in the schoolyard. George Corby would stage a photograph and then rush to get in it himself, relying on a timer or coaxing someone to snap the shutter for him. These buggies would soon be replaced by automobiles, making school outings and adventuring into the lake country much easier.

INTRODUCTION

The legend endures that the Finger Lakes were created by the Great Spirit having pressed a hand against the earth. Since there are 11 lakes, he would have had to use both hands, with Conesus Lake being his check mark of approval.

The formation of the lakes was actually the result of the last ice age, when this part of the planet was shrouded in a mile-thick sheet of ice. As the earth warmed, the ice sheet fractured. Torrential spill-offs and melt-offs lubricated huge sections of ice, causing them to slide and shape our present landscape. Some collided in stupendous explosions, spewing ice into the atmosphere like volcanoes. It is believed these fire and ice eruptions, together with violent ice-age storms, redirected the jet stream and further altered the earth's climate. Massive ice chunks were hurtled toward the ocean, shearing off tops of the Appalachian Mountains and leaving them scattered along the Atlantic floor in the form of shoals. What is thought of as a gentle handprint may have been more of a desperate clawing. The fragmented glaciers left moraines, deposits of stone and debris in the form of elongated hills. Sparkling glacial waters backed up behind them, thus forming the lakes.

Today it is a favorite tourist area noted as much for its wineries as its natural beauty. Charming towns, winery tours, resorts, lake recreation, and arts festivals increasingly draw visitors from around America. A land of monasteries and mansions, its rich history includes a United States president, abolitionists, women's rights activists, Mark Twain, aviation, and superb universities.

Several years ago, while working on Arcadia Publishing's *Around Lima*, I was shown a collection of remarkable photographs of the area taken between 1910 and 1920 by Lima resident George Bentley Corby. Like a pirate dazed by opening a long-buried treasure chest filled with jewels, I knew I had something valuable. Some of the pictures were used in *Around Lima*. This book takes a long mesmerizing look at them.

The photographs offer a view of the Finger Lakes' scenic beauty before commercial and residential development. Collectively they offer something more valuable and mysterious. They show a coming-of-age of young folk during the formative and turbulent decade of 1910–1920, when America was transformed from a rather ordinary nation into a mighty industrial and military power—the result of foreign entanglements that ultimately lured us into World War I. The last vestiges of the Victorian era slip away as America develops its own forward-looking providence.

Through Corby's photographs of farm labors, school chums, and small-town life, we are somehow constantly aware of the Finger Lakes. They beckon us like welcoming hands to their safe solitudes, there to be inspired, comforted, educated, and encouraged. Through poignant and often zestful photographs of sweet brotherhood, college days, and wartime, we are shown the importance of love of family, tradition, and how family and friends are supportive in times of joy and sorrow.

The decade saw unprecedented artistry in America. Incomparable music, art, literature, and architecture transformed us as much as war. Artists created superior products often with inferior tools. That was no less the case with Corby. Somehow he willed himself through the lens of his camera, imbuing images with virtue, personality, and sentiments his equipment could not capture. It is doubtful there is another local collection that so totally and vividly captures the everyday life of that era.

Corby, a charismatic and intelligent man, was the product of an elegant and industrious family. He took thousands of photographs, virtually of everything because, in his heart, so much in life was worth remembering. He arranged his albums with a quiet legacy in mind, probably so he could view them in his declining years to recapture the vitality of youth. We cannot, after seeing this slice of Americana, explore the Finger Lakes and ever see it the same way again. The author appreciates the assistance provided by Elaine Engst, director and university archivist at Cornell University, and Catharine Corby Gardner for use of her great-uncle's photographs. Some photographs from other sources have been included.

One

BULLY TIMES

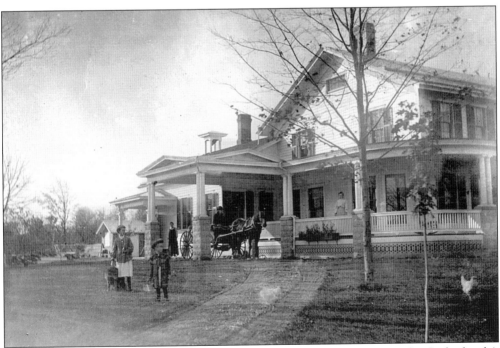

Chickens have the run of the lawn in this 1910 photograph of the George Bentley Corby family's elegant Federal-style house in Lima. It was built in the early 1800s (possibly earlier) by Asahel and Polly Birchard. Oscar and Estella Corby acquired the 240-acre farm from a subsequent owner in 1899 and named their new dairy farm Meadow Brook. They added the wraparound Colonial Revival porch. The bell in the Italianate tower, sitting atop the woodshed, dates from the 1850s. Asahel purchased the original 160 acres in 1793 when Lima was known as Mighell's Gore. Before automobiles, a comfortable day's outing to the three minor lakes—Conesus, Canadice, and Hemlock—could be made with a horse and buggy.

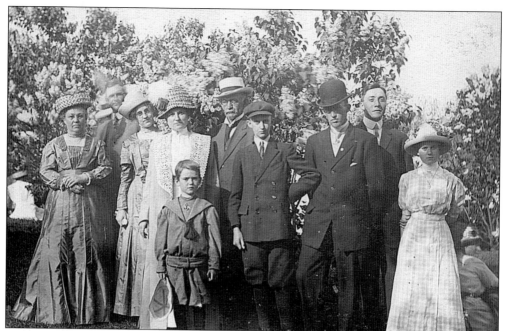

In *Family Gathering*, taken in 1911, the Corbys are visiting Highland's lilacs in Rochester. They are richly attired in clothes that bridge two eras. The older women wear taffeta dresses with elaborate hand embroidery and attachments more typical of Paris matrons. Little Bruce Corby (center) is wearing a sailor's blouse. These are holdovers from the Victorian era that is about to end abruptly with the coming of World War I. Marian Corby—at far right—wears a checkered gingham dress showing an emerging American approach to fashion.

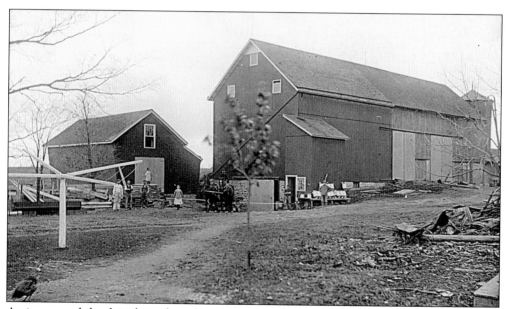

A view toward the dairy barn dates from 1910. In addition to producing milk for the Rochester market, the Corbys would later raise quality Holstein cows. Barns like these were great places to hold barn dances and corn roasts throughout the county.

In between farm and school labors, George Corby, pictured here when a teenager, took and processed hundreds of photographs at a time when cameras were a rarity. He was born on January 13, 1895.

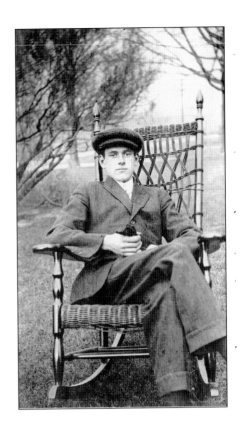

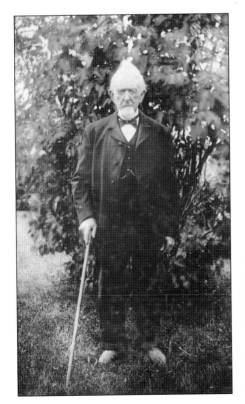

Abner Bushman, George Corby's great-grandfather on his father's side, was born in 1821. He was an active and prosperous farmer from his youngest days. Corby (above) photographed him at Meadow Brook Farm on May 31, 1913, when the strong-minded patriarch was 92 years old. The Bushmans arrived in America from Cowes, England, in 1753. One of them, Henry Bushman, fought with General Hood during the War for Independence.

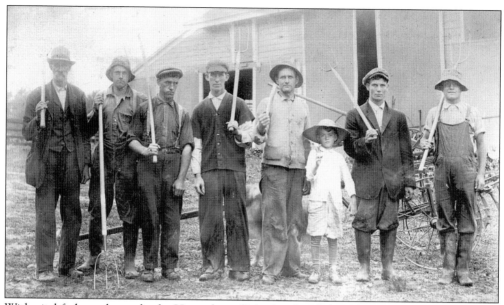

With pitchforks at the ready, the *Haymakers of Meadow Brook* dairy farm look like soldiers ready to march off to war. Oscar Corby and sons Bruce and George are included. When farmers were done with their hired help, they often leased them to other farmers. These worker cooperatives helped keep expenses down.

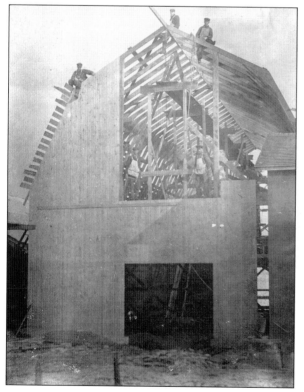

A growing dairy business with an expanding Rochester milk market necessitated the construction of larger barns. This rare view of actual barn building was taken on December 24, 1910. Not even Christmas Eve would slow things down.

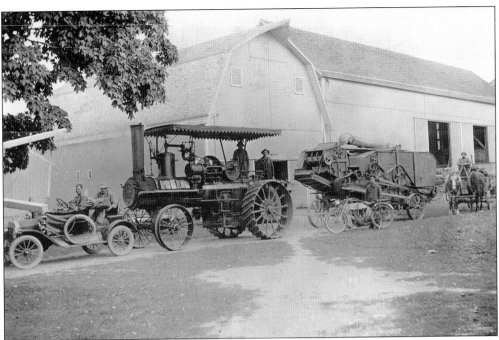

A pageant of Meadow Brook's motive power is displayed along the drive. There is a gas-powered automobile, a steam tractor, a thresher (separator), a motorbike, and a horse-drawn wagon.

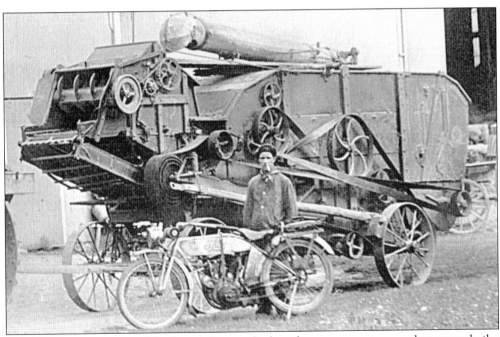

The separator was powered by long belts attached to the steam tractor or other steam boiler system. Wheat, oats, or rye were fed into the conveyor, and the stalks agitated so that the seeds would shake loose. The early motorcycle is essentially a heavily brazed-up bicycle with a gas-powered motor.

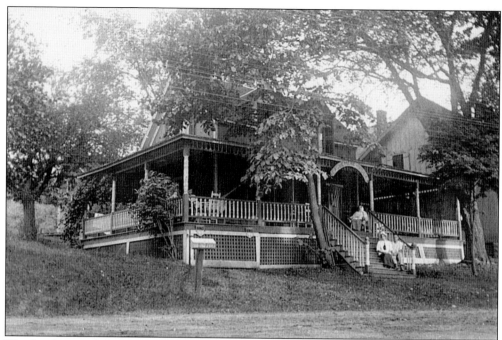

The family rented this cottage on Conesus Lake from August 26 to September 9, 1912. George Corby wrote of those days that they had "bully times."

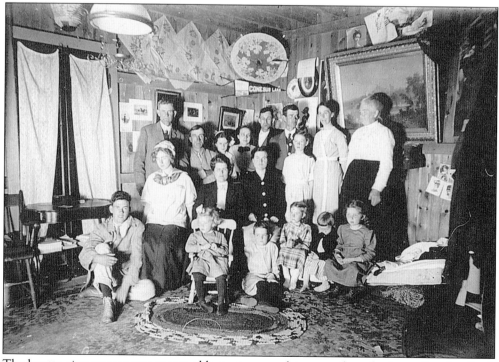

The knotty-pine cottage was roomy, able to accommodate more than the immediate family. A photograph was taken before everyone tucked in for the night.

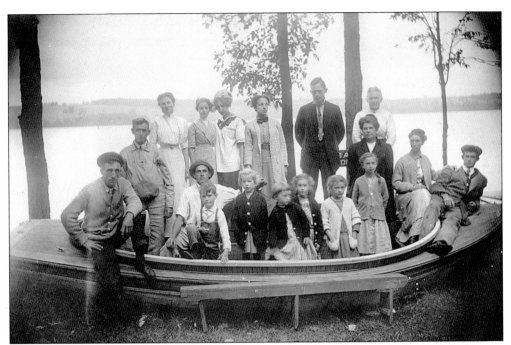

A group photograph is taken in and around an old fishing boat with Conesus Lake as a backdrop. Conesus is the westernmost lake. It is eight miles long and has a maximum depth of 66 feet. Camps, cottages, and resorts lined its shores even back in 1912 when this photograph was taken.

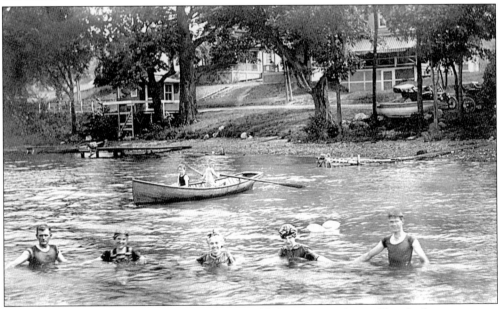

A dip in the lake followed by boating, fishing, and hiking were welcomed breaks from strenuous farm labor. Conesus, Hemlock, and Canadice Lakes were the three minor lakes, sometimes called the Three Sisters. They did not draw as much attention as the larger eastern lakes, but the locals did not seem to mind. They worked their grape farms, carried on lake trade, ran steamers to resorts, and lived in a quiet isolation.

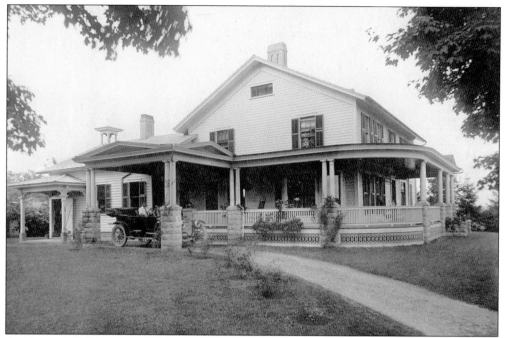

A side view of the Lima farmhouse shows the carriage port occupied not by a horse and buggy, but by that remarkable new invention—the automobile. The freedom and adventure it offered was exhilarating and life altering.

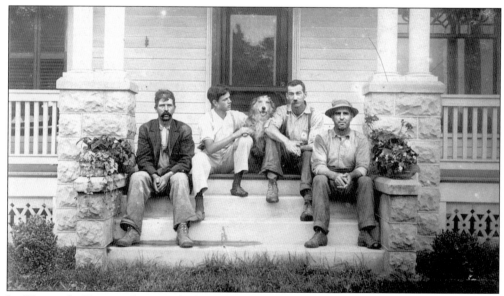

In *Waiting for Dinner*, photographed on the front steps, fatigued workers are waiting for the dinner bell to clang from the tower over the woodshed.

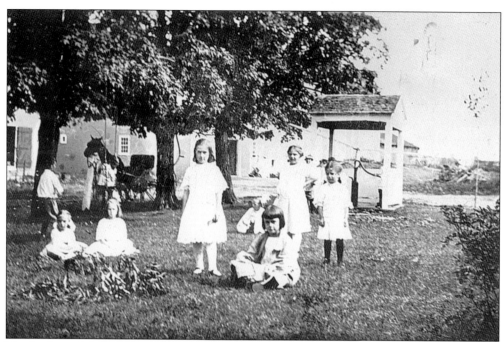

Neatly dressed friends from Honeoye Falls and Lima are arriving for Bruce Corby's birthday party being held on the side lawn. They will enjoy games, pony rides, cake, and homemade ice cream.

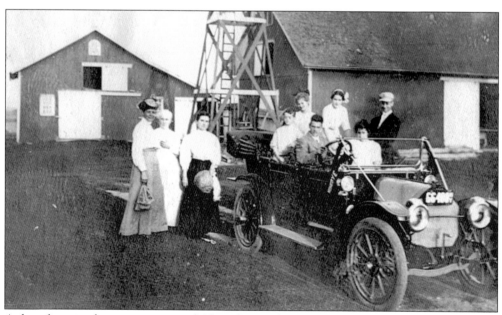

A day of touring has come to an end. Note the crank on the front of the car. Before electronic ignitions, the spark was set by manipulating two levers on the steering wheel and the crank was given a few harsh turns to get the motor turning. It could be dangerous business. Sometimes the kick of the motor would throw the crank backward, resulting in a bruised arm. Another interesting artifact is the windmill back near the barns. It was used to draw water from the well.

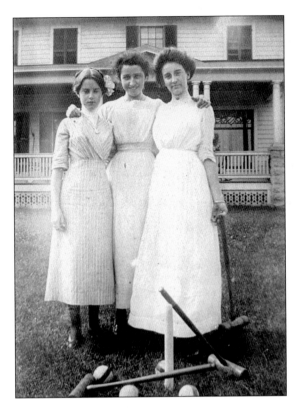

Croquet mallets and balls have been carefully arranged to bring a sense of balance to this photograph. From left to right are Marian Corby, Edna Davis, and Etta Root.

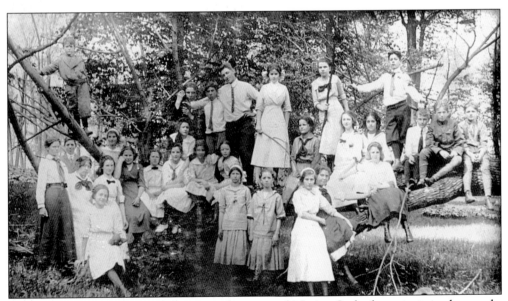

Friends from town and around the county have joined Marian Corby for a picnic in the woods.

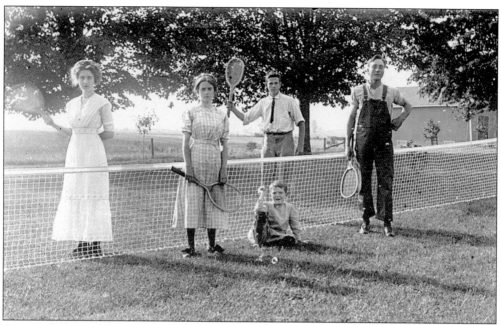

Among the lawn games played at Meadow Brook and other farms were tennis and croquet. From left to right are cousin Ida Filkins, Marian Corby, George Corby (behind the net), Bruce Corby (sitting), and Charles Fellows.

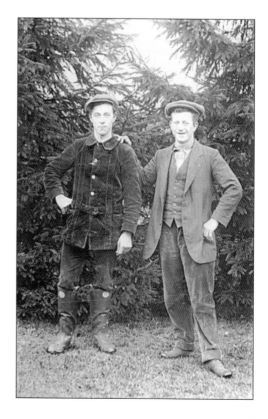

In this photograph, titled *Dutch Chums*, Pete and John, who had some association with the dairy farm, pose expressively.

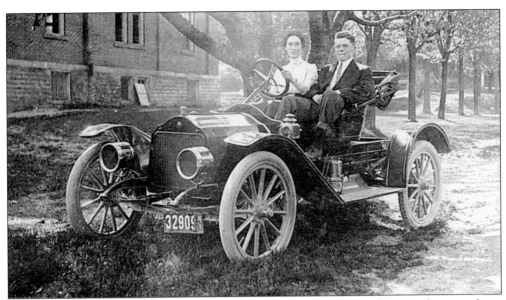

A young lady takes the wheel of one of the first horseless carriages to clatter and sputter down Honeoye Falls' streets. The 1911 photograph was taken beside Harry Allen School. The steering wheel is on the right side. This motor buggy had some extras such as acetylene headlights and generator instead of oil lamps, and an extra set of small oil lamps mounted to the fenders. The three-bow top (convertible top) was detachable. The body of the car was shiny black, and the wheels and chassis may have been dark carmine or Brewster green.

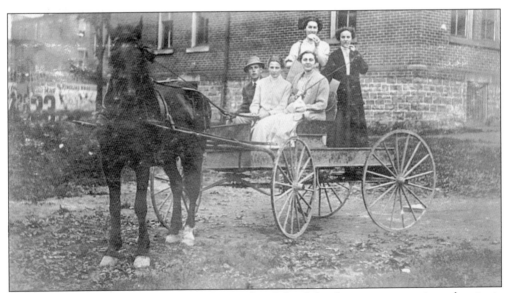

Attendees to a baseball game behind Harry Allen School decide its time to get into the picnic basket for some sandwiches in this snapshot taken on May 29, 1911. It would be a while yet before buggies faded completely from the scene.

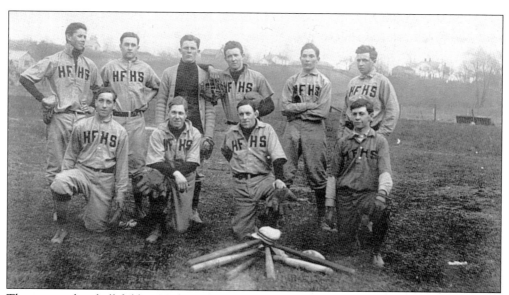

There was a baseball field in Hyde Park in the village of Honeoye Falls that got a lot of use by schools and locally sponsored teams. In this April 1911 photograph, the Honeoye Falls High School team strikes a determined pose.

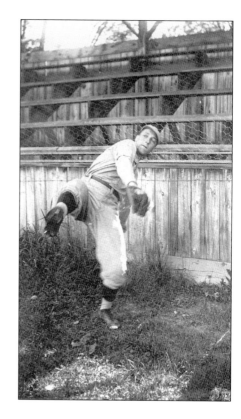

The pride of the school's 1911 team, Harold "Wizard" Mattern, shows off his powerful pitching windup.

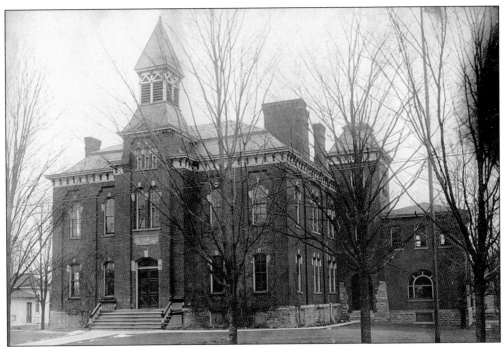

Honeoye Falls Union Free School was built in 1879. It was enlarged in 1896 and renamed Honeoye Falls High School. At that time there were seven teachers—earning an average of $9 a week to handle approximately 320 pupils.

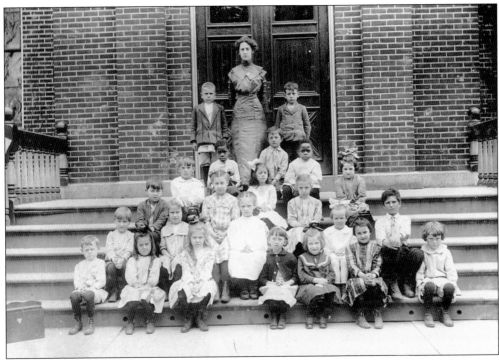

The first-grade class of 1911–1912 poses on the steps of the school on May 7, 1913.

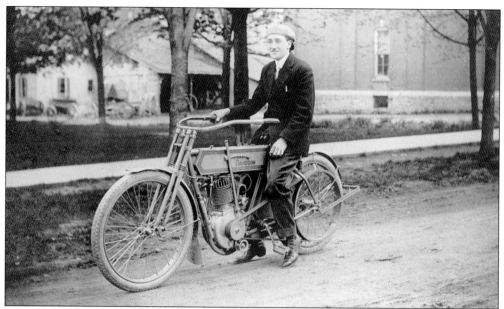

A sensation in its day, this *c.* 1912 Harley Davidson turned a few heads while grumbling along village streets. The evolution from a motorized bike to an actual new species—the motorcycle—is evident in the heavy-gauge brazed-up tubing construction. It could reach 25 miles an hour but had terrible hill-climbing abilities. There was no transmission. Speed was controlled by using the large lever to increase or decrease tension on the belt drive.

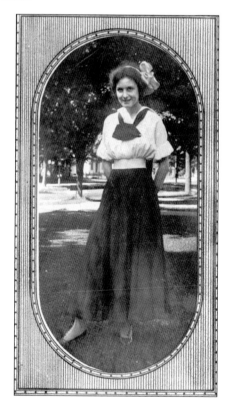

Demure and sweet, Marguerite Keyes, a friend of George Corby, was photographed on May 27, 1911, on a shady Honeoye Falls street.

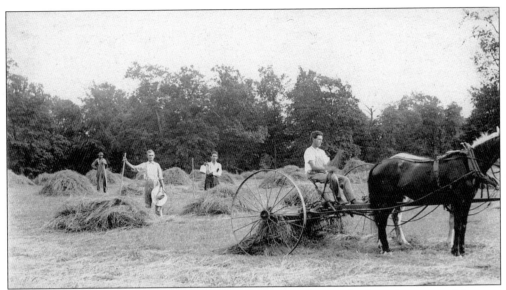

It is haying time. Hay is being raked and bundled to be taken to the barn for storage. Honeoye Falls and Lima were part of America's original "bread basket" before that distinction was wrested away by Midwestern states. Honeoye Falls gristmills ground quality flour that was sold in Europe. Village streets were often congested with wagons of produce from Lima farms waiting to be shipped via train to locations along the New York Central's Peanut Line branch.

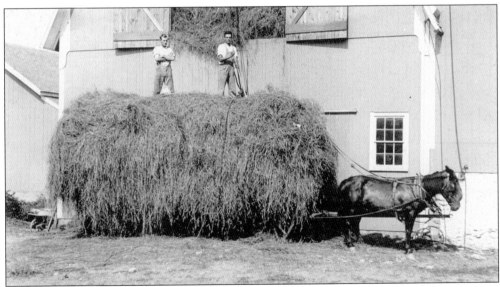

A dray burdened with hay has pulled along Meadow Brook's new barn. Oscar Corby and son George are on top with pitchforks preparing to pitch it into the hayloft.

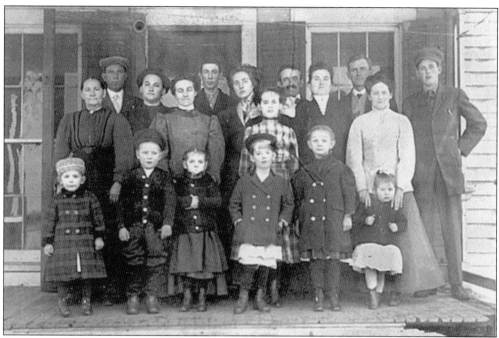

In a photograph titled *The Reeves Crowd,* a young George Corby shows his talents for composition. The Reeves were on his mother's side. The older women show a straight-backed pioneer determination. The new generation seems well looked after. Young Bruce Corby is in the middle front. Marian Corby is behind him, and George is to the far right. Below is a similarly strong image. *The Simmons Reunion* finds three proud generations on the stone steps of a handsome residence.

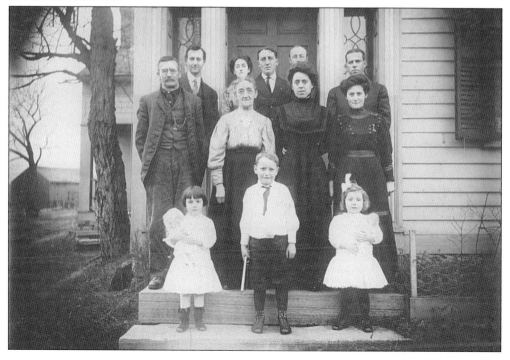

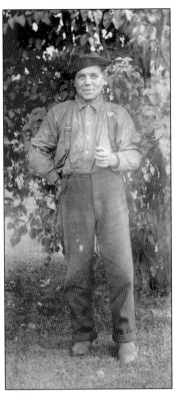

With pipe in hand, farm laborer Billy Van de Mark seems relaxed as the young photographer snaps his picture. The Dutch started moving here in the early 1770s, some escaping the manorial tenant system of Dutch patroonships along the Hudson Valley.

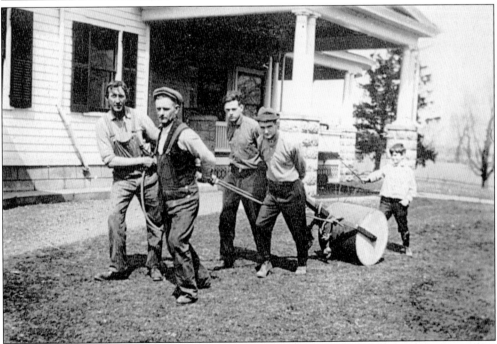

Spring rolling will even out irregularities in the lawn caused by winter's heaving frosts. The farmhouse and grounds were impeccable, rivaling the elegant homes of landed gentry in surrounding counties.

Farmhand Dix stands at the back corner of the house in the diminishing shadows of late day. He has a kind face. A typical day would include milking cows, mucking stalls, and getting milk containers to the railroad station for the Lehigh Valley's morning milk run.

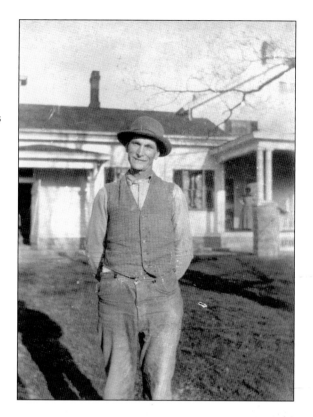

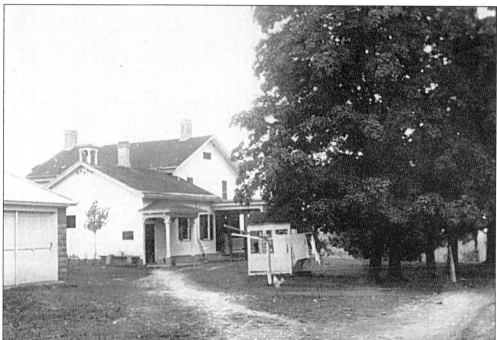

A closer look at the woodshed with its 1850s Italianate bell tower is provided in this photograph. The clothes rack and pump house have survived to this day.

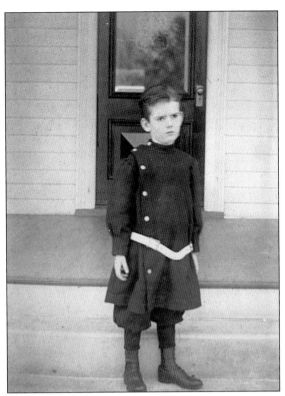

Bruce Corby looks less than pleased in a fussy "Little Fellows" sailor suit. Made of wool and cotton, it was oppressive on hot days. Things look better below. Shoeless and with Meadow Brook's acres waiting beyond him, he looks ready to spring from the steps; a Huckleberry Finn off to find Tom Sawyer.

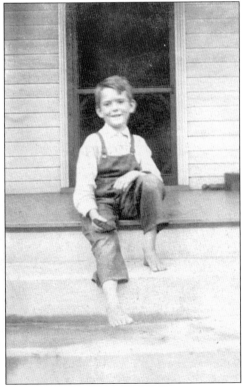

Marian Corby contemplates her long hair on a sunny March morning in 1911.

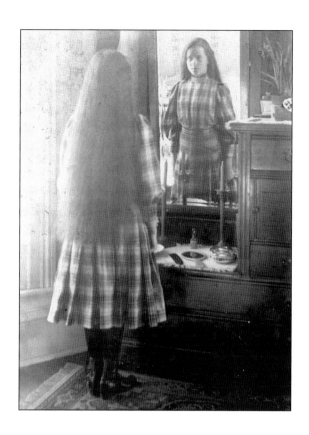

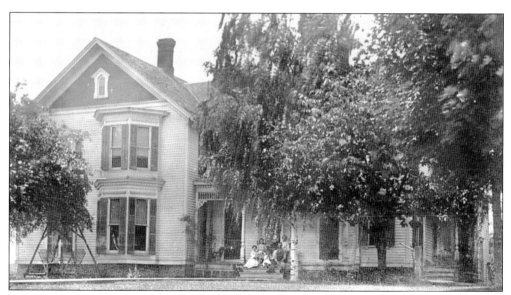

Before moving to the farm in Lima, the Corbys lived in this home on Clover Street in Pittsford for a while. They are on the porch in this photograph, taken during a visit to the home.

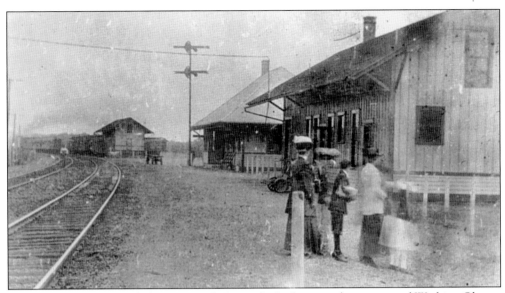

Three stations comprised the New York Central's facilities at the summit of Watkins Glen, a favorite tourist stop at the south end of Seneca Lake. It is late in the day, and passengers are awaiting trains back to Rochester or points south. The departing train has just moved on to a tall bridge over the gorge.

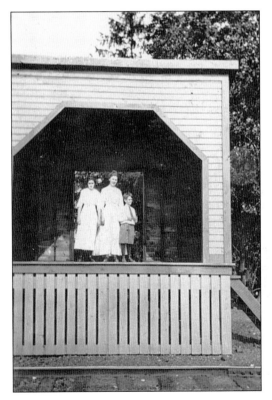

Marian Corby, Estella Corby, and Bruce Corby are standing on the platform of a milk station, a seldom-photographed structure once common along railroad branches and spur lines. The elevated platform made moving the heavy metal milk containers into the refrigerator cars easier. The roads leading to milk stations usually dipped down. Wagons and then trucks would back down so that the back of the vehicle was level with the platform, again making it easier to move the containers.

Two

A WINTER'S SPELL

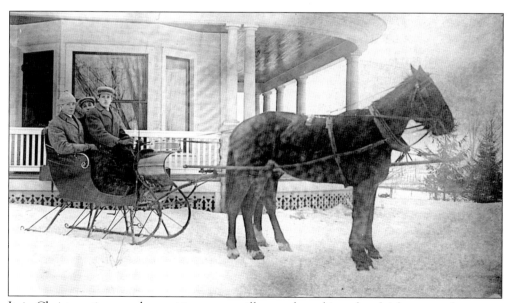

It is Christmastime, and a waiting team will soon be taking the sleigh across the snowy countryside. If gift shopping were the objective, a stop at Beadle Brothers or Sangers in Lima would yield toys, clothes, jewelry, books, magazines, or tools.

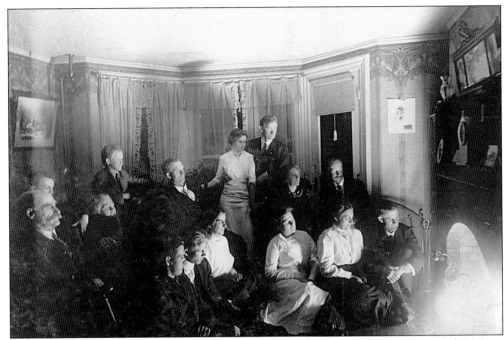

The warm glow from the fireplace illuminates family and friends in a photograph titled *A Merry Fireplace Circle*, taken in the front parlor.

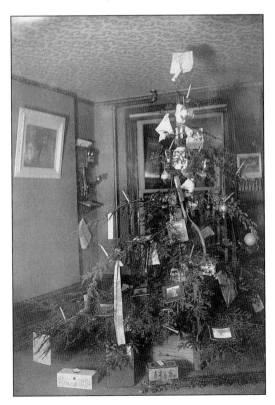

The Christmas tree is ready for the yuletide celebration. Gifts and a cast-iron train are arranged beneath the tree. Decorations include glass balls, ribbons, a tennis racket, and not surprisingly, photographs. The candles were carefully—and briefly—lit Christmas Eve night and again on Christmas morning.

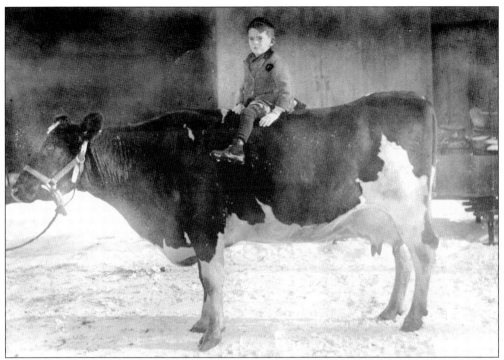

Bruce Corby was patient with his older brother's persistent photograph taking. Here he waits atop a dairy cow until his brother takes his photograph on a chilly day in December 1910.

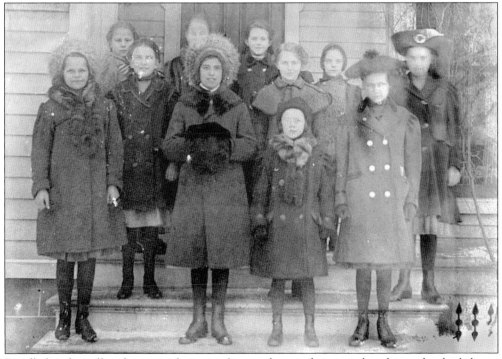

Bundled in fur-collared coats and wearing hats and caps of many styles, these schoolgirls brave the cold while George Corby gets his photograph.

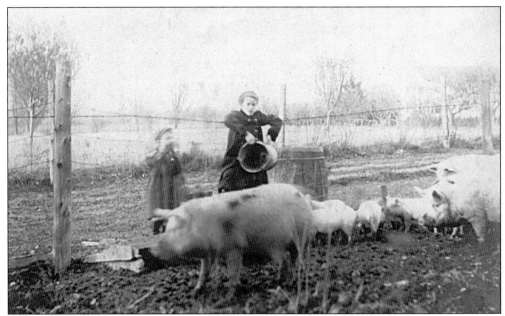

It was not all pretty clothes and lawn parties at Meadow Brook. Children were expected to do their fair share of farm work. Marian Corby seems astonished that her brother just took a photograph of her and Bruce Corby slopping the hogs on this cold morning.

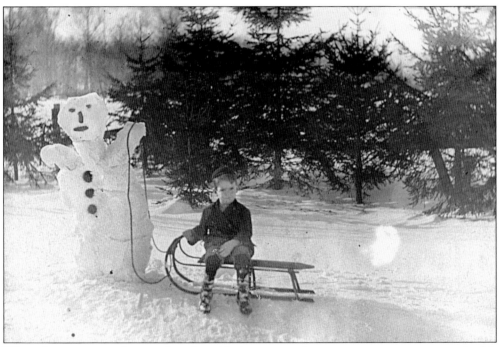

When there were no pals around to play with, it was sometimes necessary to create one as in this photograph titled *Bruce and His Friend*.

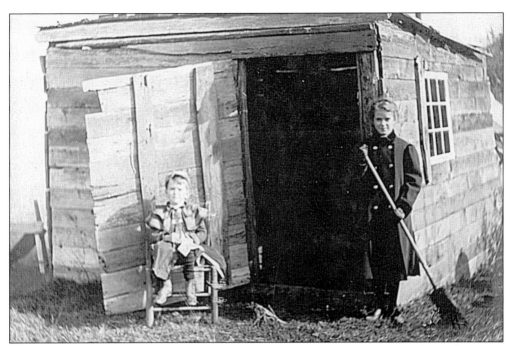

Bruce and Marian tidy up a barnyard shanty. Hours could be spent playing here with friends. Although a crude structure, to adventurous-minded children it could become a royal palace, a fort, or a *Treasure Island* hideaway.

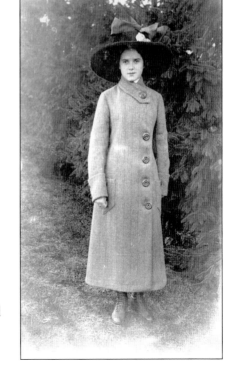

Marian seems quite mature in her large buttoned wool coat and enormous wide-brimmed hat. The crown of the hat is a tam-o-shanter with giant flowers and ribbons attached. Similar high-fashion hats had names like Ravina, Superba, Shereton, and Bramford. Little misses spent hours perusing the fashion sections of the Sears catalog and magazines of the day.

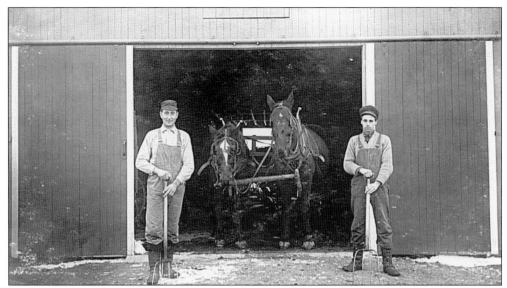

Farmhands stand like sentinels guarding a palace doorway in a photograph titled *Ready for a Load*.

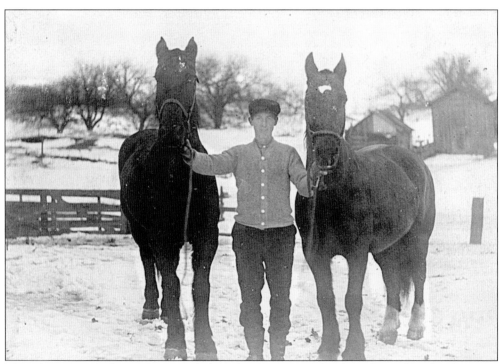

These horses in *Uncle Joe's Team* are believed to be Morgans bred at a horse farm heading west out of Lima on the old State Road. There was a Percheron breeding farm in nearby Bloomfield.

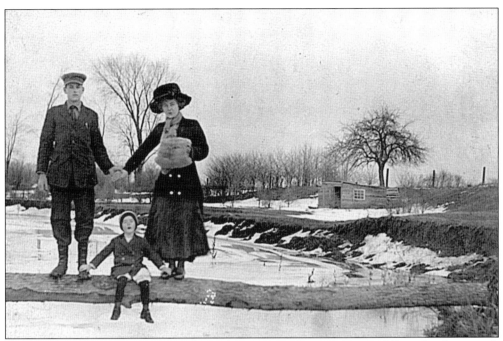

Cousin Ida Filkins joins Bruce Corby and George Corby on a log straddling the farm pond. Among the winter recreations were hiking, skiing, and certainly ice-skating and hockey on that pond.

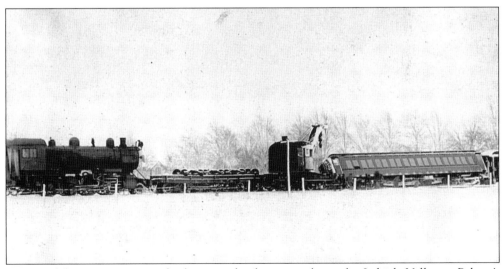

A crane lifts a passenger car back on track after a wreck on the Lehigh Valley at Palmer's Crossing. The Lehigh ran a branch from Rochester through Lima and down to Hemlock Lake. Its primary customer was PINCO insulator in Lima, although it picked up milk and produce from Lima farms.

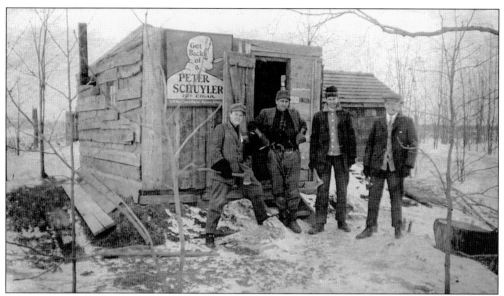

Members of the *Round Up Gang* stand outside their den, a backland shack where farmhands could take breaks, warm up, cook, and spend the night warmed by a wood-burning stove.

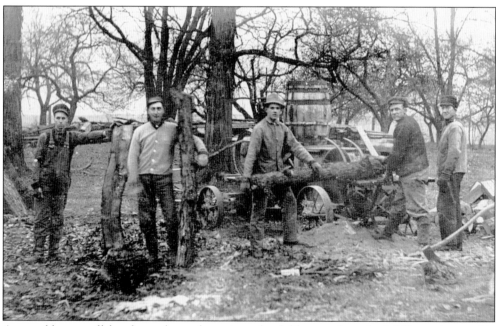

A portable sawmill has been dragged out into the fields to reduce dead falls to sizes usable in stoves and fireplaces. The water barrel suggests the mill was steam powered. Farmers often fabricated their own equipment—usually with a little help from the local blacksmith.

The upward tilt of spruce branches offers cousin Ida Filkins, always a fashion plate and seldom camera shy. The emergence of American fashion is evident in Ida's winter wear. Sleeker, more natural-fitting clothes were the trend. The large velvet poke bonnet and Kolinsky muff and scarf—with the animals' heads and paws attached—were all the rage. The photograph was taken during a visit to Meadow Brook.

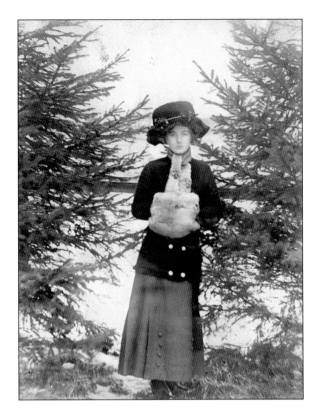

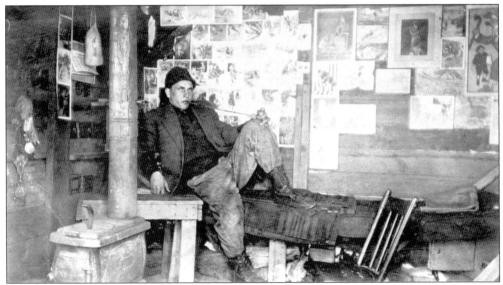

Wearing clothes soiled from a hard day's work, the *Captain of the Round-up Gang* reclines contentedly in his den. His long clay pipe will provide additional enjoyment during his night in the rickety outland shack. The walls are covered with illustrations from magazines of the day. Farmhands were rarely photographed, but George Corby felt them worthy. He used his camera to exalt people and never to shame them.

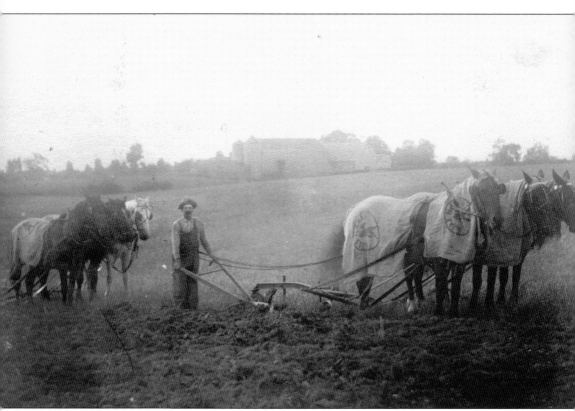

Mist-laden fields glisten on a spring morning. It is planting time, and plowmen have their horses ready. The horses are blanketed against the early morning chill with stitched-together flour sacks. In the distance are the dairy barns.

Three

RITES OF PASSAGE

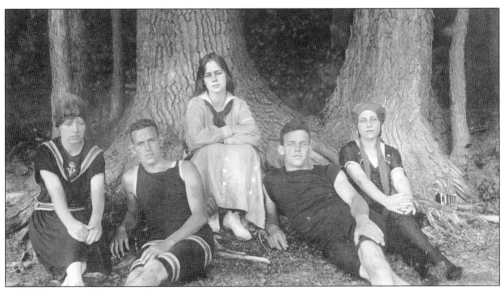

The decade of 1910–1920 saw America transformed from a rich but timid nation to a major superpower. The collapse of the Old World that had emerged after the Napoleonic Wars led to World War I. America watched apprehensively the crumbling of the Ottoman, Austro-Hungarian, German, and Russian empires. Inevitably America would be drawn into the conflict. George Corby and his friends would be called upon to settle things and would do so at great expense. The Finger Lakes was, to many of them, a place to come of age. Pictured from left to right are Thalia, George Corby, Emily, Chief, and Helen.

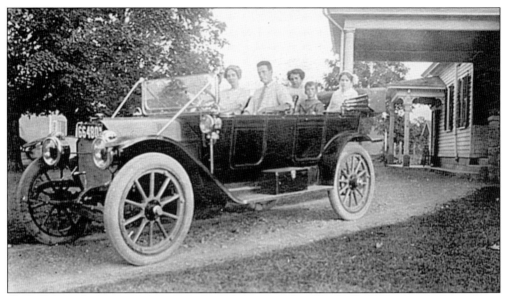

Outings into the Finger Lakes region were more comfortable in this larger touring car. There is a toolbox fastened to the running board. Early cars needed constant maintenance, and it was up to the owners to learn basic repair mechanics. It was good to have a copy of *Dyke's Automobile and Gasoline Engine Encyclopedia* in the box along with some Seroco Waterproof Auto Top and Seat Dressing, Seroco Cup Grease, denatured alcohol, and an extra pair of four-lens automobile goggles.

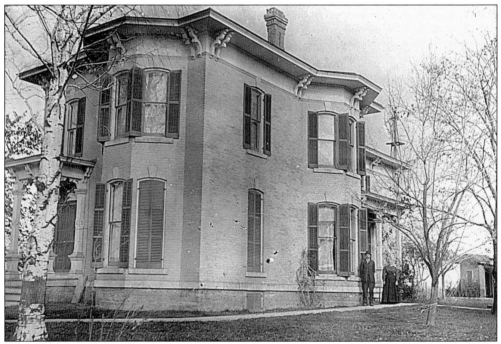

This handsome brick residence was home to George Corby's grandparents Frank and Georgia Corby. It stands in Honeoye Falls on Main Street, just up the hill from Hyde Park. An elaborate porch and porte cochere were added later.

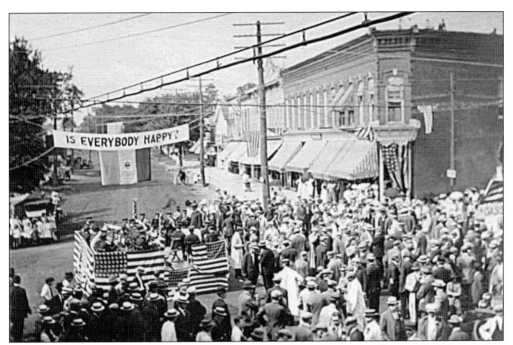

The Rochester Chamber of Commerce sponsored a rally in Honeoye Falls around 1913 complete with a band, refreshments, and exhibits.

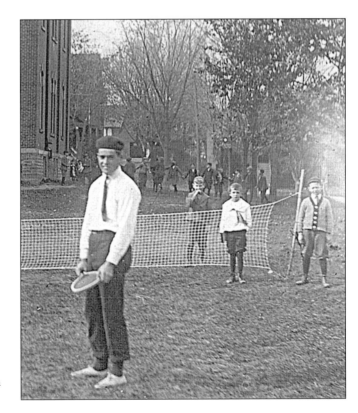

Neighborhood kids take turns at tennis on the grounds behind Harry Allen High School.

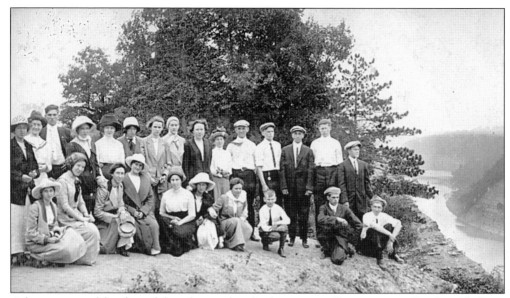

A large group of family and friends pose beside the gorge at Portage—now Letchworth State Park—during an outing in 1913. Some of the women wear hats with auto scarves and veils. They could be pulled around their faces to protect them from road dust while driving. Most of the men are sporting linen golf caps.

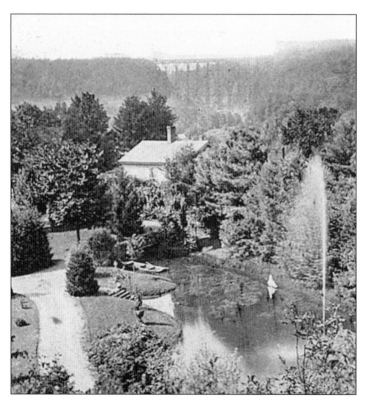

A view from the early 1870s shows Glen Iris, William Pryor Letchworth's home at Portage, with its pond and fountain. In the distance is the spectacular 820-foot wooden trestle that carried the Erie Railroad over the gorge. The photographer of this stereo view is unknown.

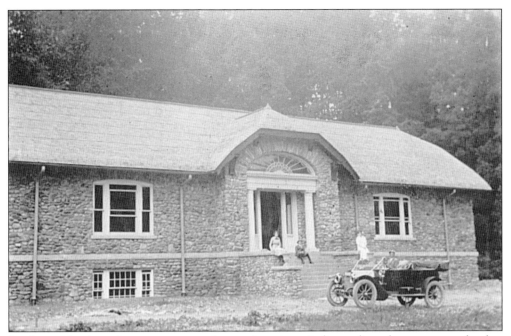

Letchworth's plans for a museum to house American Indian relics, documents, and other collections were realized shortly after his death in 1910. The impressive stone structure has just opened in this 1913 photograph. The remains of a mastodon dug from a farm near Pike, New York, and a bench from Hornby Lodge would be among its most noted attractions.

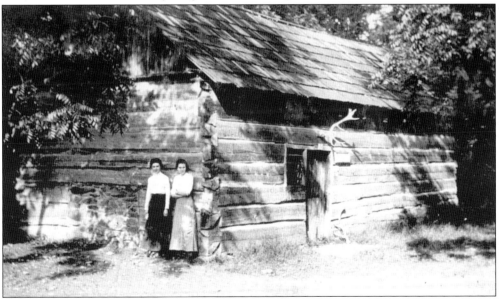

This c. 1780 Seneca council house originally stood at Canadea, New York. Letchworth purchased the sad ruin and had it restored on a plateau near Glen Iris. The new council grounds would hold the remains of Mary Jemison, "the White Woman of the Genesee," whose captivity and life among her adoptive American Indians is legendary. An impressive statue of her is at the grave. The cabin she built upriver at Gardeau was also moved here. Letchworth hosted the last council fire of the Iroquois at Glen Iris in 1872.

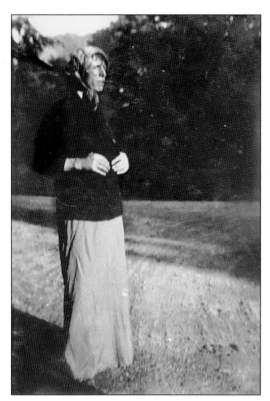

Gradually the Iroquois faded from the edges of fields where whites purchased their crafts or hired them at planting and harvest times. They either moved on to reservations or assimilated into the white man's society. George Corby photographed this American Indian woman near Glen Iris. Her face and hands tell of years of hard work. Her simple homespun skirt conveys a kind of pride. Unmistakable in the old woman's gaze is an abiding for her people.

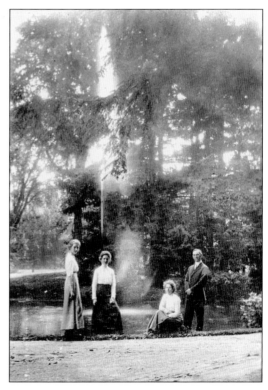

The fountain at Glen Iris rises into the morning mist behind this group during a visit to Portage.

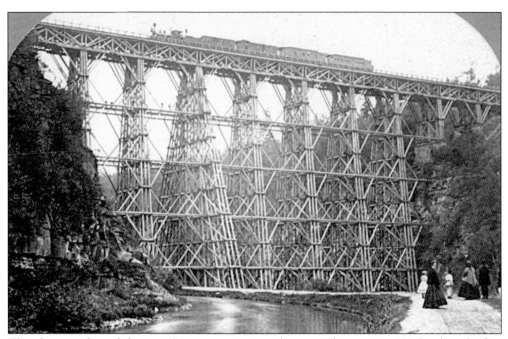

The photographer of this *c.* 1870 stereo view is unknown. The massive 820-foot-long bridge, built in 1852 by the Erie Railroad, soared 235 feet above the gorge. It caught fire on May 7, 1875, and burned in a spectacular blaze for almost a week. Visitors saunter along the towpath of Genesee Valley Canal that curved under the bridge.

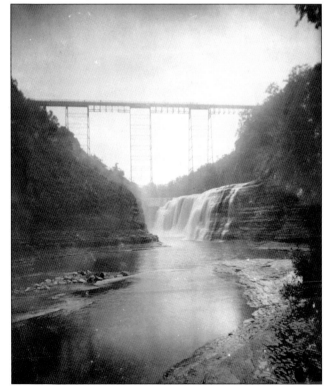

The iron replacement bridge, constructed quickly after the destruction of the wooden trestle, led to speculation that the Erie Railroad management had deliberately torched the original bridge because it could not handle the traffic. The Genesee River and falls beneath the bridge glimmer in George Corby's photograph.

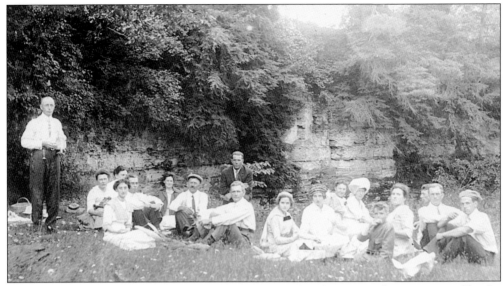

Tourists relax at Fall Brook along one of the Portage trails. The spectacular gorge carved by the Genesee River in its northward flow to Rochester is called the Grand Canyon of the East.

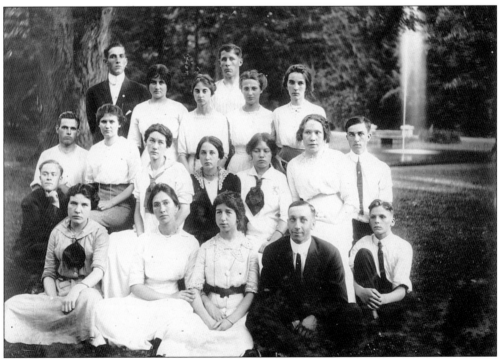

The largest graduating class of Honeoye Falls High School, class of 1913, is photographed at the fountain and pond at Glen Iris.

A dry spell has reduced a waterfall near Moscow, New York, to a trickle, but enough water remains in the creek basin for reflections of Marian Corby and her friend.

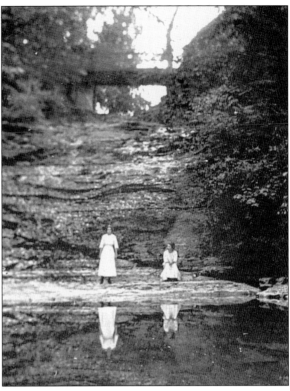

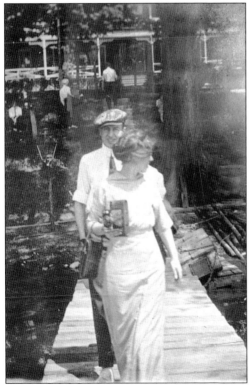

Classmates Vince and Michie approach the *Jaeger* tour boat during a high school picnic at Conesus.

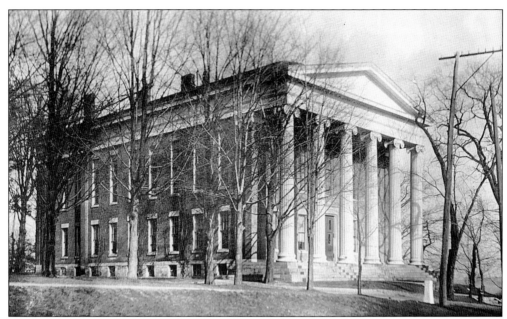

In 1830, the Conference of the Methodist Church selected a hilltop in Lima for their Genesee Wesleyan Seminary campus. It made Lima an important educational center in New York. In 1849, the seminary created Genesee College, a companion college. The main facility for that institution was College Hall, pictured here. After several difficult years, the trustees of the struggling college decided to relocate the college to Syracuse. George Corby attended the seminary in 1913 for a year of undergraduate study.

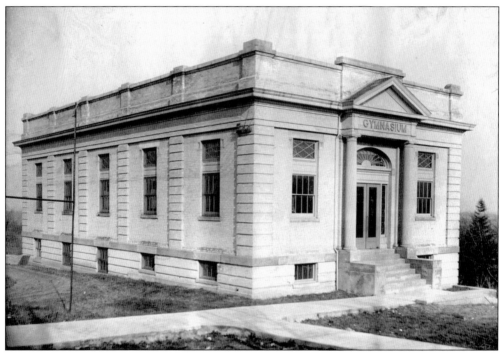

The seminary's classically styled gymnasium served students for several generations.

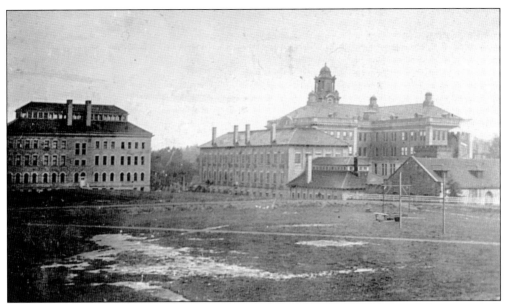

A class trip to Syracuse University yielded a view of the "Old Row" above, and the university's sports field below.

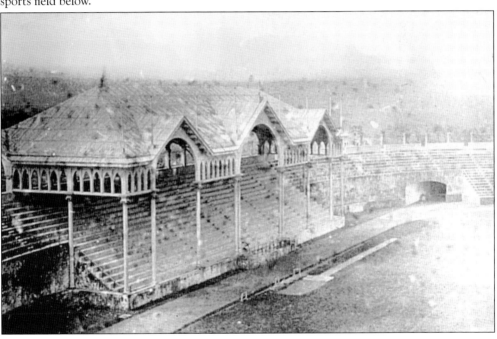

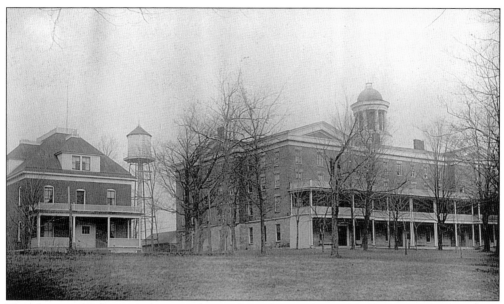

The Genesee Wesleyan Seminary's dormitory, with its columned bell tower and verandas, is to the right. Faling Hall is to the left. Among the noted alumni to attend Genesee Wesleyan Seminary were Sen. Kenneth Keating; Henry Raymond, publisher of the *New York Times*; and Belva Lockwood, the first woman to run for president. The campus was purchased by Elim Bible Institute in 1950. In 1951, it began classes as a bible and missionary school, continuing a long tradition of coeducational excellence.

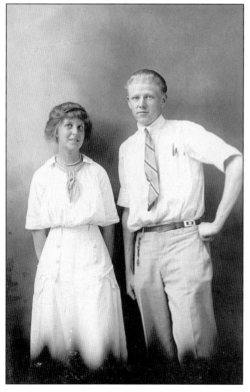

Two seminary students from George Corby's circle of friends pose against a photographer's backdrop. The title is *Van's First Skipping*.

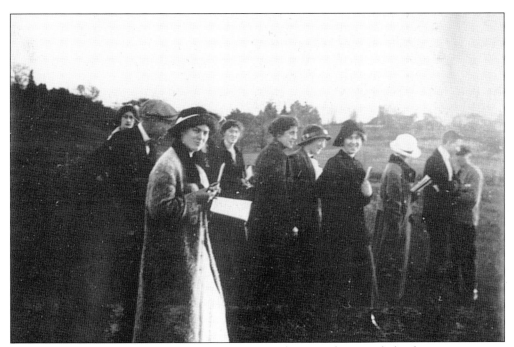

Like Druids during a celestial ceremony, seminary students conduct a twilight physics experiment on the campus to test velocity of sound in air.

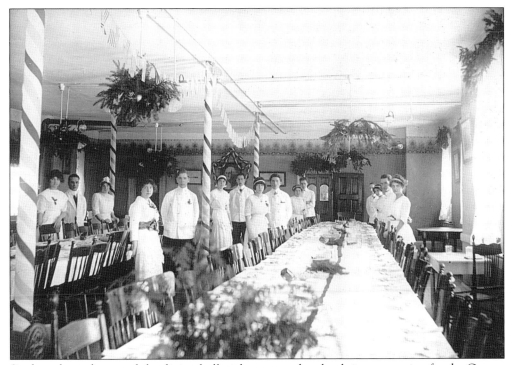

Students have decorated the dining hall with crepe and garlands in preparation for the George Washington banquet.

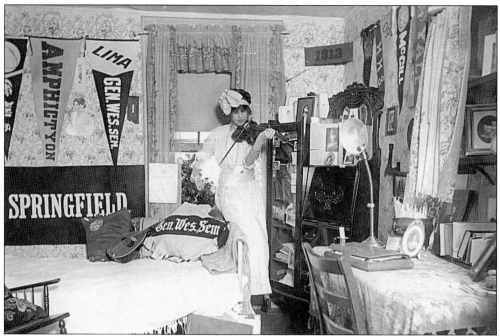

Ruth Williams plays her violin in her campus room in the girls' dormitory. A profusion of pennants adds liveliness to this 1913 photograph.

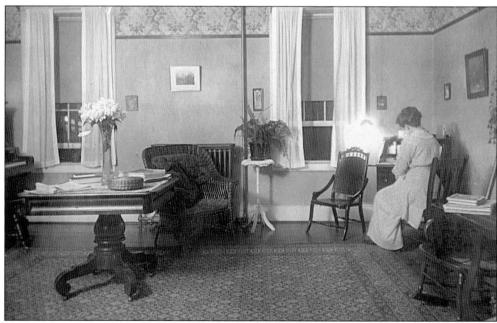

The simplicity of *Miss Bernhard's Parlor* suggests she used the room to receive small groups of students, possibly for music recitals. She pens a letter at her desk. The illumination of the lamp was "burned" during film processing to intensify its glow.

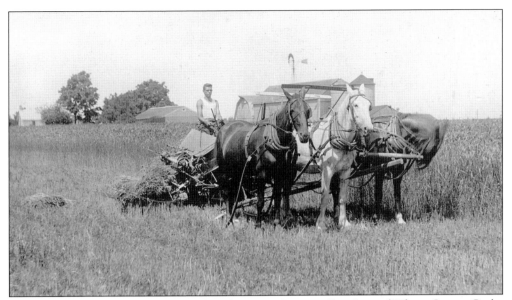

Schoolwork offered no reprieve from farm duties. In *Cutting a Fine Piece of Wheat*, George Corby operates an old-style self-raking reaper. Genesee Country wheat, among the finest in America, had to be cut at the right time or it would loose seeds in the field. These machines, which were prone to breaking down, at least had interchangeable parts and could usually be repaired on the farm.

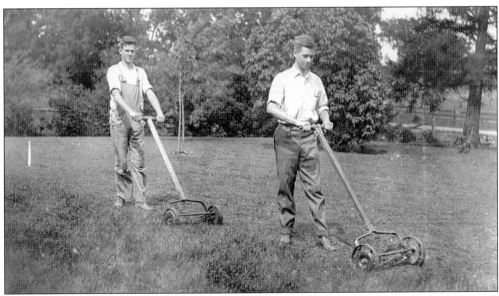

The sprawling lawn around the home at Meadow Brook required regular mowing with push mowers. Here Corby gets help from his cousin Albert Root.

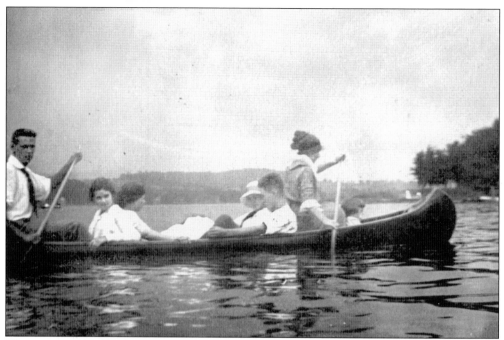

Weary rowers head back to shore after a day of sun, fresh air, and canoeing on Conesus Lake.

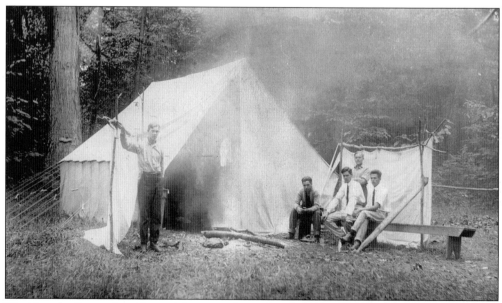

The Baracca Boys, a local boys club, warm themselves by a morning fire during a camping trip at Honeoye Lake. Some of them are wearing ties. It looks as if a neat appearance was expected no matter what the event.

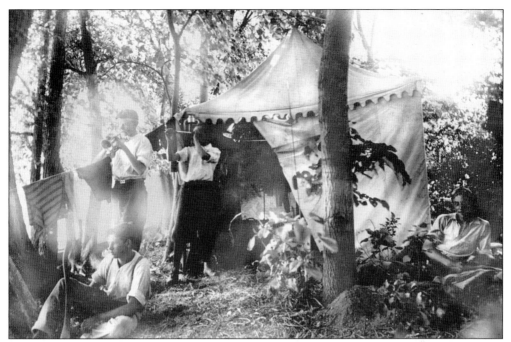

Adventurous camping in the woods was made even more exotic in this Arabian-style tent. The boys have with them a bugle, a telescope, fishing poles, oars, a hatchet, and an oil camp lantern.

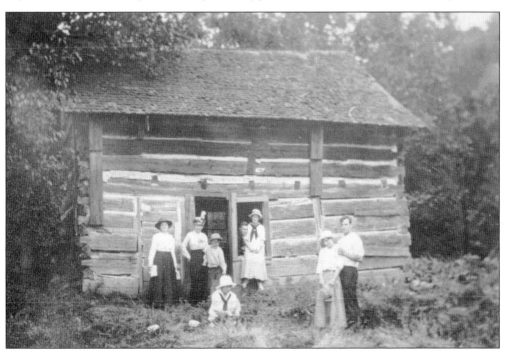

It is believed Gen. John Sullivan spent a night in this cabin during the Sullivan Expedition in 1779. The massive offensive into the Finger Lakes region chastised the Iroquois for depredations against white settlements and for allying with the British. The cabin was located on a trail between Conesus and Hemlock Lakes.

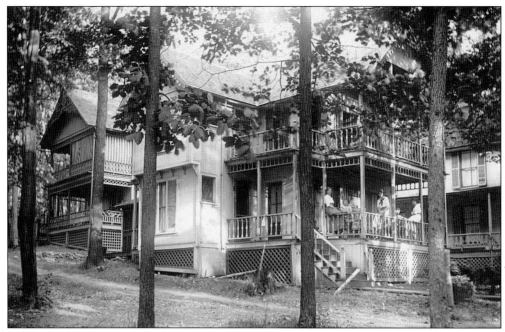

In *Thurston's Cottage*, a lovely Victorian structure is dappled in noonday light. A tightly packed neighborhood of these is situated along Silver Lake—not officially a Finger Lake but located along the chain. Family and friends of the photographer relax in the cool shade of the two-story veranda.

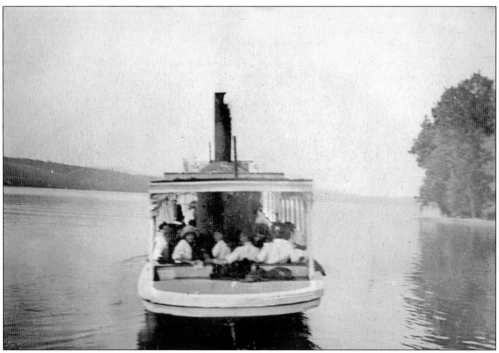

In *Farewell Conesus*, students head back to the steamboat landing after a day of touring the lake.

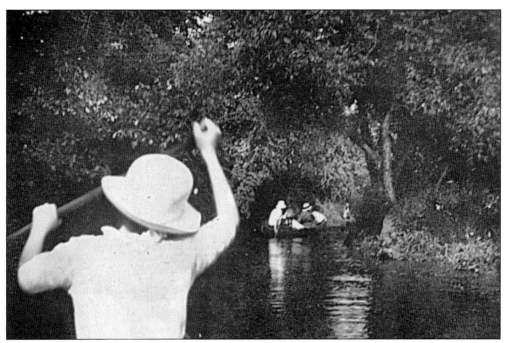

A hot sun beats down on Silver Lake as friends paddle toward the coolness of the lake's shadowy outlet.

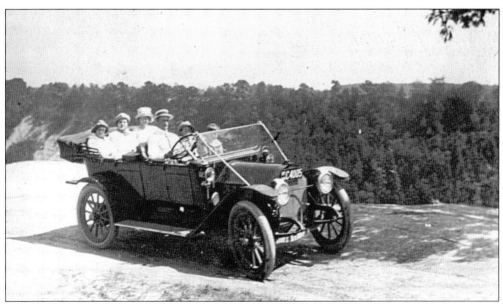

These tourists are on the road to Silver Lake. As roads were improved to accommodate increasing numbers of automobiles, sleepy towns began to spruce up to cater to tourists. The number of fill-up stations increased. Many were converted blacksmith shops. Tobacco, snacks, and full lunches were usually available at them. Rental cottages and campgrounds were developed along with fashionable Victorian inns and modest motels. Resorts with tour boat landings were particularly popular.

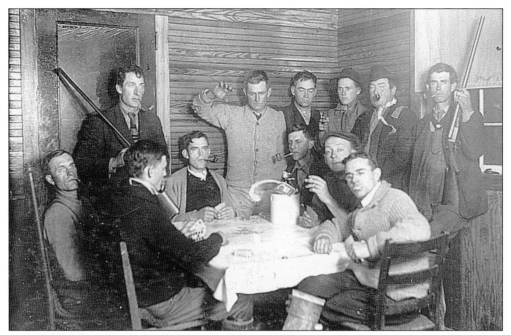

In *A Wild Night at Hemlock Lake*, these well-dressed fellows are thoroughly enjoying themselves in a hunting cabin. There is a card game going on, and a jug of liquor is making the rounds. Opinions about the kaiser and the war were probably expressed more colorfully than when women were present.

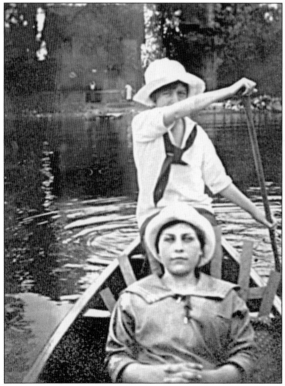

Classmates Thalia (rowing) and Helen are out for a boat ride along Hemlock Lake during a school picnic. Hemlock was once a popular resort. The Lehigh Valley Railroad brought tourists, including trainloads of PINCO employees, for daylong picnics. Hemlock and Canadice Lakes were acquired as water supplies for Rochester, which severely restricted shore development and recreation.

A compelling portrait of Ethel, a Genesee Wesleyan Seminary student, shows George Corby's ability to capture virtue with his camera.

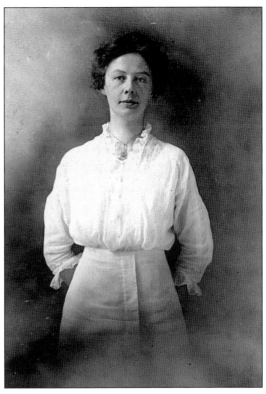

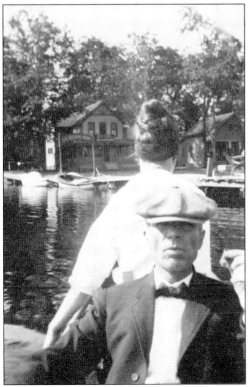

The etiquette of the time required the accompaniment of chaperones at student picnics, dances, or other socials. Giving chaperones the slip was regularly attempted.

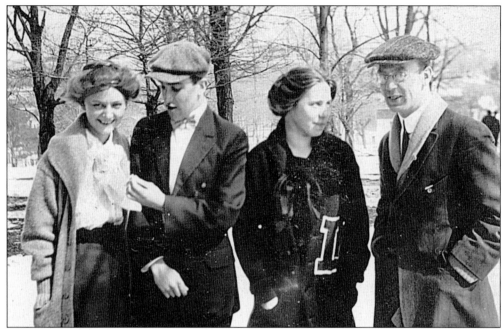

Seminary students at the hilltop campus on a wintry day are the subjects of musings in a photograph titled *The Saddest Cases*. Up until December 1914, they could take the Lima-Honeoye Falls Light and Railroad trolley to Honeoye Falls to attend dances and roller-skating parties.

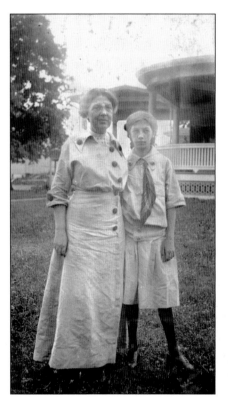

Cousin Margaret Root and daughter Ellsworth, wearing a cotton sailor's suit, are visiting Meadow Brook from Kansas.

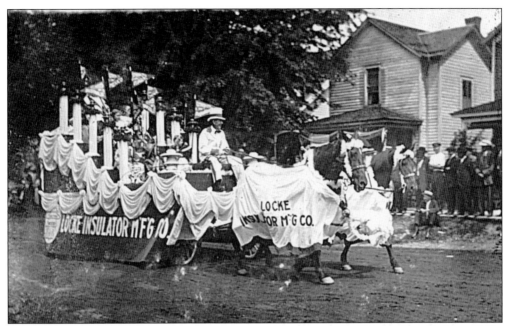

This lavish float was part of the parade celebrating the centennial of Victor, New York, in 1913.

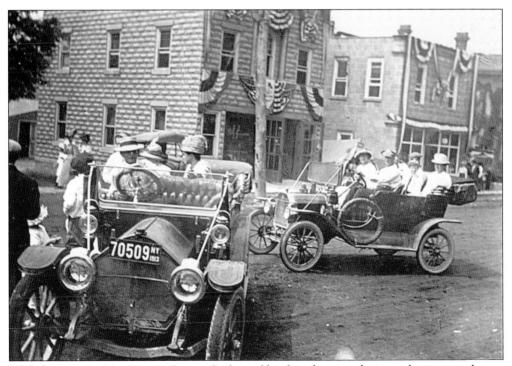

With festivities in Victor over, George Corby and his friends swing their runabouts toward more adventures. The automobile brought a thrilling sense of freedom to these young folk.

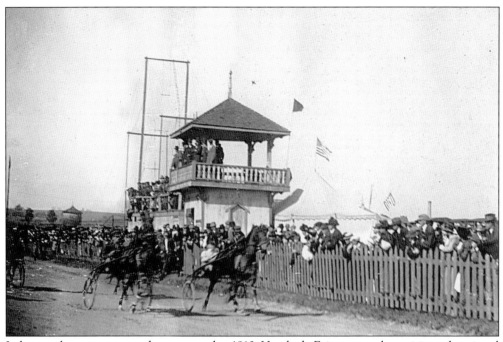

Judges and spectators watch races at the 1913 Hemlock Fair—a much anticipated regional event. Along with races and other competitions, prized livestock and the latest farm equipment were exhibited.

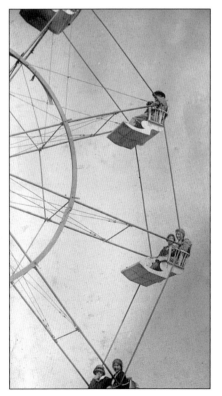

The Ferris wheel was among the more popular amusement rides at the fair.

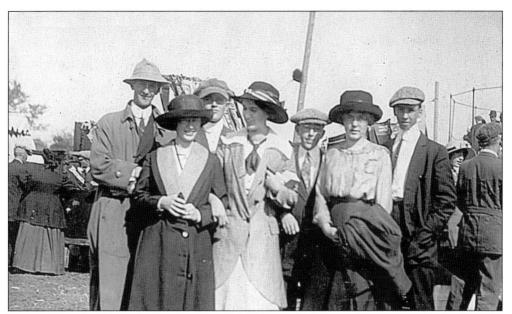

These well-dressed friends—or sports, as they often called themselves—are making a day of it at the fair. There were other county and firemen fairs, but the Hemlock Fair was always the best and remains popular even today.

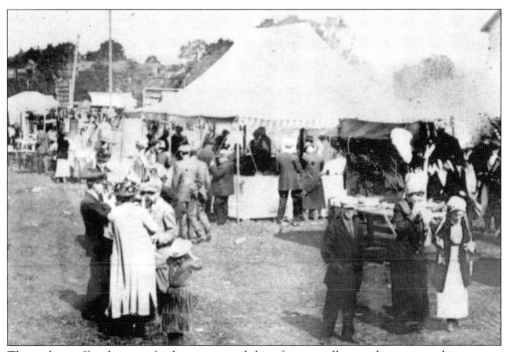

The midway offered games, food, company exhibits, fortune-tellers, and exotic wonders.

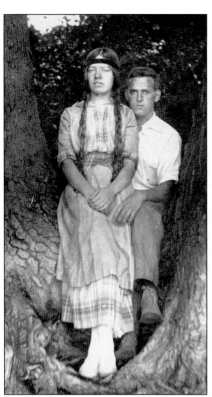

Thalia and George Corby are seen during a class picnic at one of the lakes.

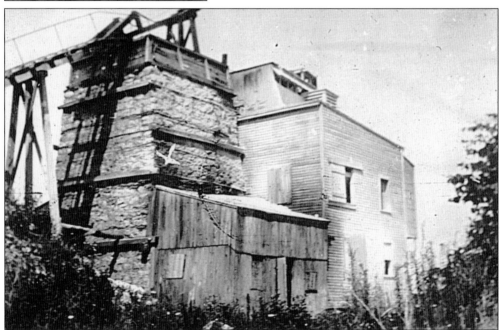

Genesee Lime Kiln, located off Dalton Road in Lima, New York, produced quicklime, a by-product of limestone fragments burned in the stone chamber. The by-product was essential to the production of lime mortar, which was used to build many of the fine cobblestone structures in the greater Rochester area.

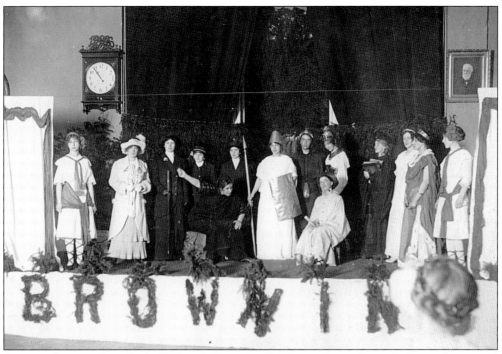

A scene from student Ruth William's *Browning Public*—a short classical play with a moral message—is performed on the auditorium stage in College Hall.

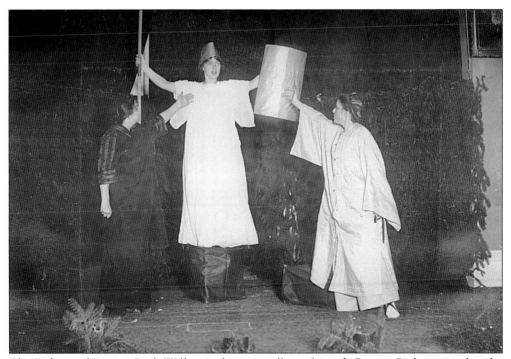

The *Epilogue of Farce* in Ruth William's play is grandly performed. George Corby writes that the girls from left to right are "Monty's girl—Vince's—mine."

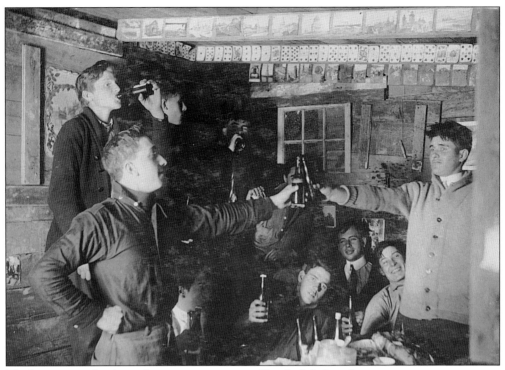

The boys raise a few beers during a stay over at a Hemlock Lake cabin.

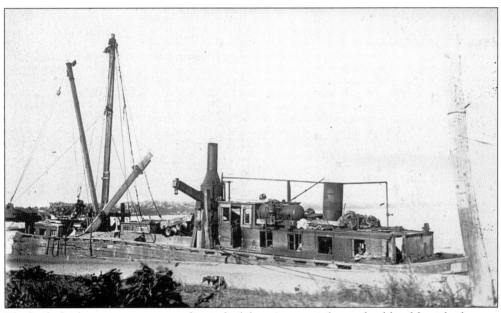

The lowly dredger was a common sight on the lakes. An ungainly ramshackle of derricks, booms, and boilers, it was a dowdy sister to the queens of the lakes, the elegant tour boats. This is the *Dr. Chapin*, a dredger, photographed in service on Seneca Lake.

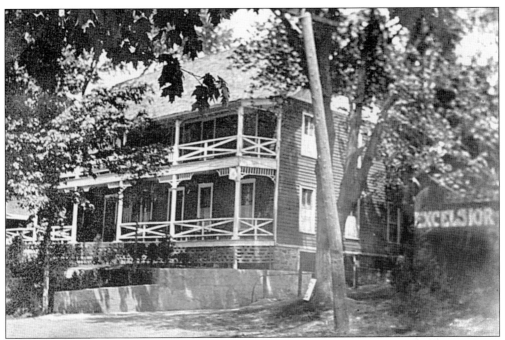

A combined Genesee Wesleyan Seminary junior-senior picnic day was held at Excelsior Springs in 1913. Dinner was held in the cottage after a day of hiking and boating.

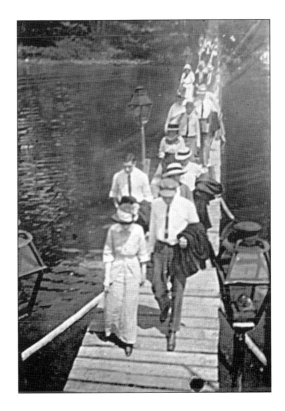

The classes are preparing to board a naphtha-powered launch for a trip out to Long Point on Conesus Lake.

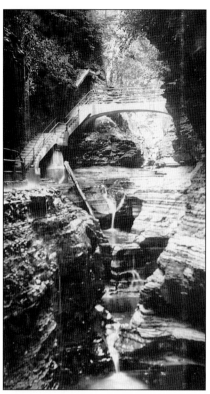

Watkins Glen is a fantastic natural wonder at the head of Seneca Lake. The 100-acre reserve features a narrow two-mile glen carved by a watercourse that makes a gradual 700-foot descent over rapids and multiple waterfalls. Pictured is the Flying Stairs at Rainbow Falls.

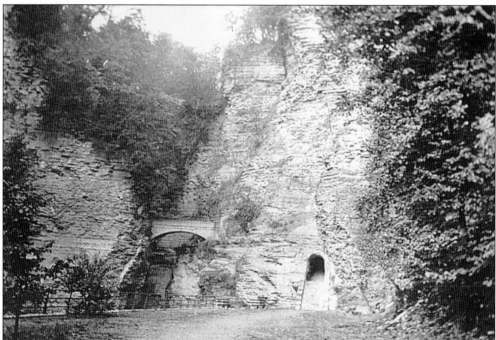

The entrance gates are located in a natural formation called the Amphitheater. The glen is located just outside the village of Watkins and was reached by a walk from the steamboat landing at Seneca Lake or by train.

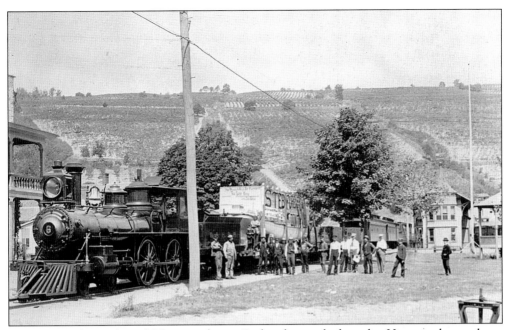

A train on the Bath and Hammondsport Railroad is parked at the Hammondsport depot at the south end of Seneca Lake. The unusual geography of the lake country made railroad construction difficult. In some cases freight was moved on boats and canals and then to rail centers. The photographer is unknown.

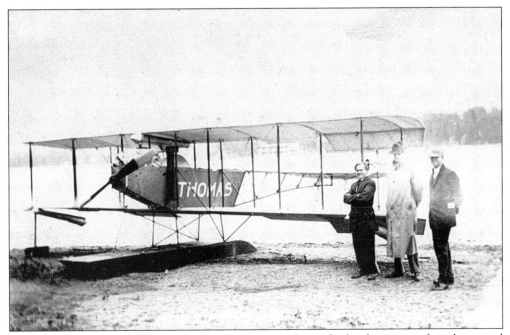

People along Seneca Lake were fortunate to witness the early developments of airplanes and seaplanes manufactured by Glenn Hammond Curtis, a former manufacturer of motorcycle engines. The military would soon be purchasing his airplanes. World War I had begun, and it was only a matter of time before America got involved.

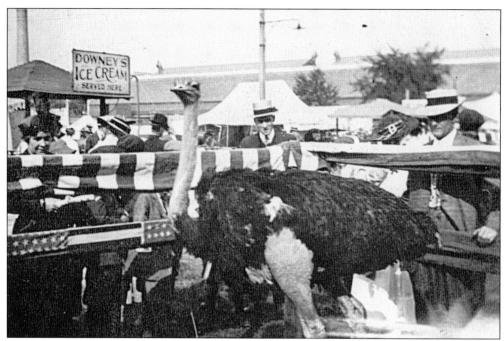

A visit to the annual Rochester Exposition provided an opportunity to observe exotic creatures such as this ostrich. The complex of exposition buildings was located on Edgerton Street, not far from the Erie Canal.

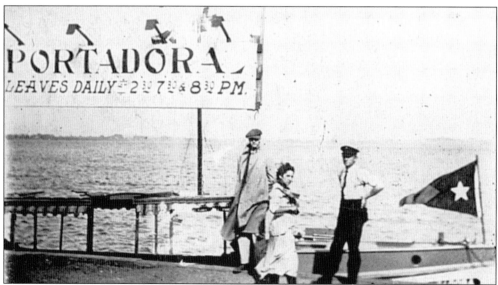

The tourist boat *Portadora* is moored at a windswept dock at Seneca Lake in a photograph titled *On Vacation with Towers*. The lake, named after the Seneca Nation of the Iroquois, is 38 miles long, making it the largest lake entirely within New York State and the second deepest in the United States at 618 feet. Over 40 wineries take advantage of the lake's unique microclimate, which allows the near-perfect cultivation of grapes.

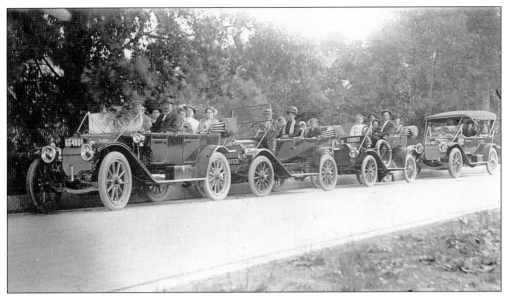

Wearing their Sunday best and with their touring cars polished, the Corbys and friends embark on a tour of Canandaigua Lake's wineries and recreation spots.

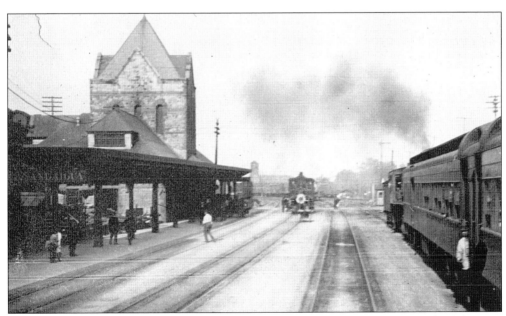

Passenger trains arrive and depart the c. 1900 station on the Canandaigua branch of the New York Central. Service between Canandaigua, Batavia, and Buffalo began in 1853 on what was called the Peanut Branch.

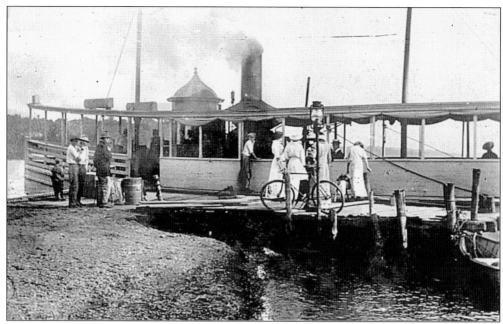

A Conesus Lake steamer awaits boarding by gracefully dressed young ladies from the seminary. A tour often included a cruise out to McPherson's Point and then Long Point. Schools, churches, companies, and other societies would charter these boats for a day. Below, three young crewmen relax and enjoy their pipes before casting off.

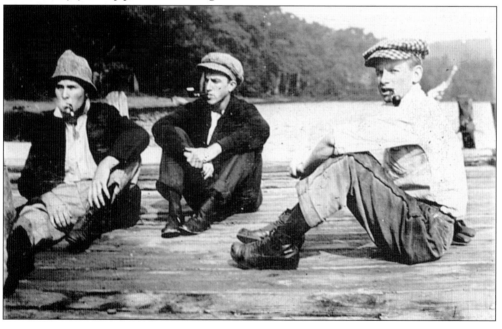

Captain Tewey, the pipe-smoking cursing master of the steamer, looks like he would not take guff from anyone. His aspect is closer to that of a steamboat captain like Mark Twain (below) than of a New England old salt.

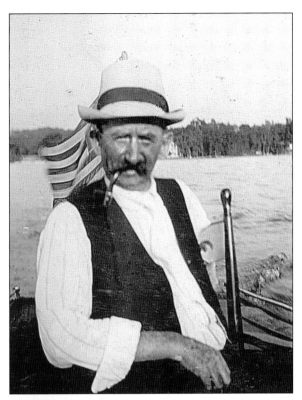

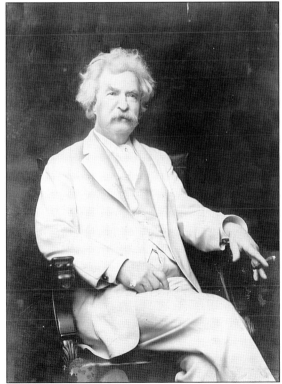

Born Samuel Clemens, Mark Twain (1835–1910) was a former steamboat captain who spent many summers at Quarry Farm, the Elmira home of his sister-in-law Susan and her husband, Theodore Crane. His family said his happiest days were spent there with his wife, Olivia, and children, four of whom were born in Elmira. It was at Quarry Farm that he did the bulk of the work on such masterpieces as *The Adventures of Huckleberry Finn*, *The Adventures of Tom Sawyer*, and *The Prince and the Pauper*. (Courtesy Library of Congress.)

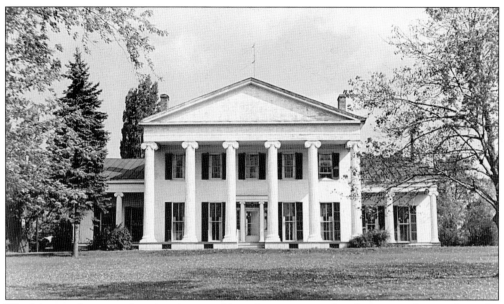

The history of westward emigration is told in the mansions, farmhouses, and inns along the old State Road (Route 5 and Route 20). Completed in 1809, it ran, in part, along the northern tips of the lakes, connecting the Hudson and Niagara Rivers. It retains much of the history, legends, and tales of failure and fortune in the lake country. Pictured is Rose Hill in Geneva, a 26-room Greek Revival mansion built in 1839. (Photograph by Elizabeth Holahan; courtesy Library of Congress.)

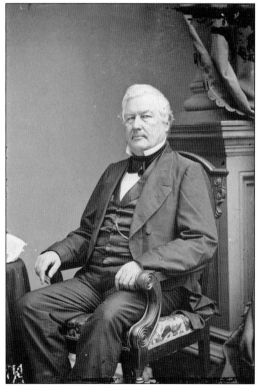

Millard Fillmore was the 13th president of the United States, succeeding from the vice presidency after the death of Zachary Taylor. He was the last member of the Whig party to hold that office. He was born in Summerhill, a small town in Cayuga County. (Courtesy Library of Congress.)

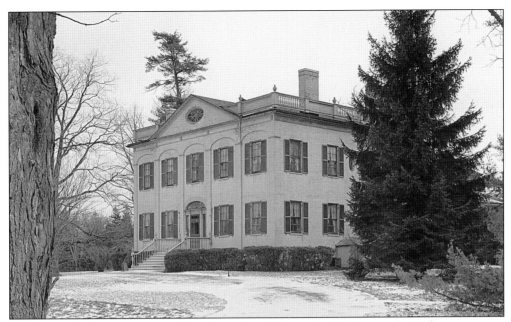

Lorenzo sits back on a generous lawn from the old State Road. The neoclassical mansion was built in 1807 by Col. John Lincklaen, an agent for the Holland Land Company. It is located in the picturesque town of Cazenovia, overlooking Cazenovia Lake, which, although not officially a Finger Lake, lies within the region containing the chain. Jack Boucher took this 1962 photograph. (Courtesy Library of Congress.)

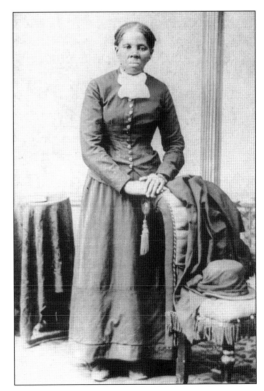

Harriet Tubman escaped slavery and became one of the most noted "conductors" on the Underground Railroad, personally helping about 300 slaves escape to freedom. She was referred to as the "Moses of Her People" and had a $40,000 reward out for her capture. She lived much of her life in Auburn and died there in 1913. This photograph is from 1880. (Courtesy Library of Congress.)

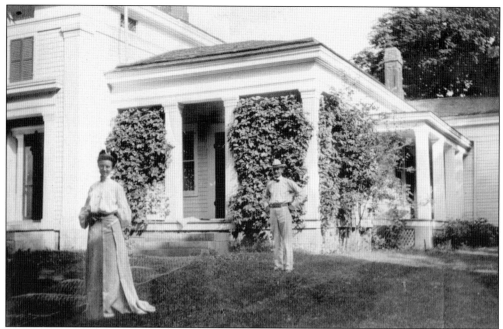

Lima, along the old State Road, has more than its fair share of beautiful residences. This fine Greek Revival on East Main Street was built in 1857 by Daniel Steel, a landowner and banker who founded Stanley's Exchange in the village. The photographer of this *c.* 1904 photograph is unknown. (Courtesy George and Fran Gotcsik.)

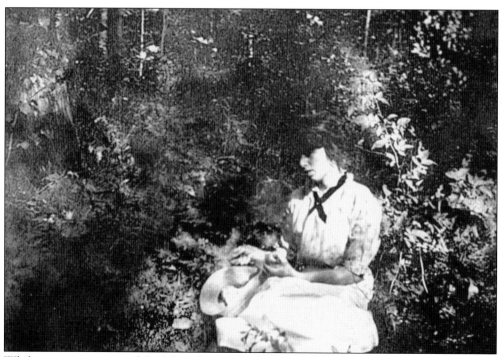

While on a visit to one of the lakes, George Corby snapped this photograph of Ruth Williams enjoying the coolness of the woods.

George Corby and Ida Filkins wait for the camera's timer to click during an outing.

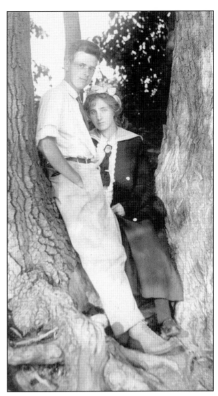

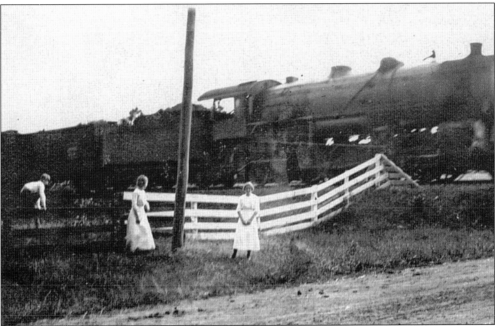

Mere humans seem vulnerable in this photograph of a Delaware, Lackawanna and Western Railroad steam engine charging through a crossing. The railroad branched through the lake country hauling mostly anthracite coal from Pennsylvania's Lackawanna Valley to connections at Ithaca, Utica, Oswego, and Buffalo.

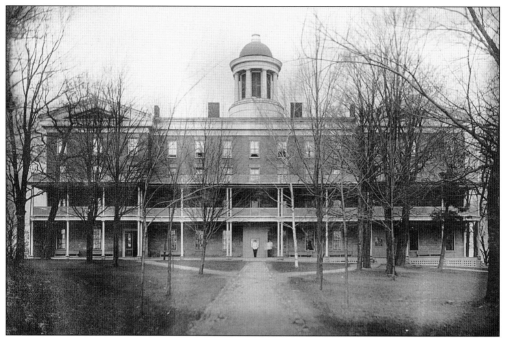

Genesee Wesleyan Seminary's campus buildings were built of brick made at brickyards along the edge of the village. The columned bell tower is still visible from miles away, particularly from farm fields.

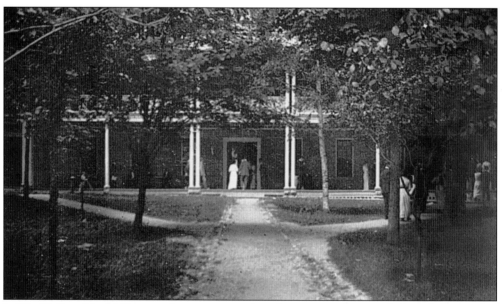

In *The Ending of Social Hour*, students return to their dormitories after a nightly twilight ritual of strolling the campus, conversing, meditating, exercising, and praying. Often it was a time when plots were hatched. After finishing homework, these students will most likely write letters home to friends.

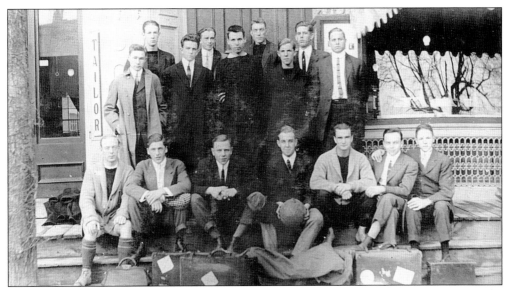

The seminary soccer team is awaiting transportation to a game. They are seated in front of the Stanley Exchange building in Lima.

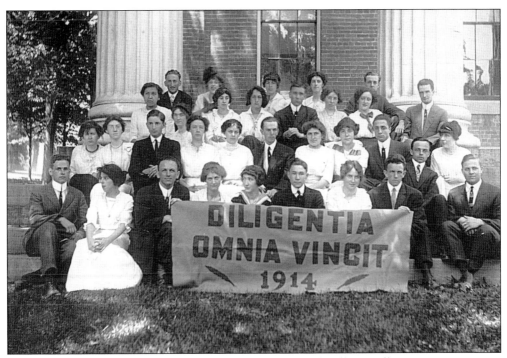

The graduating class of 1914 is photographed on the steps of College Hall.

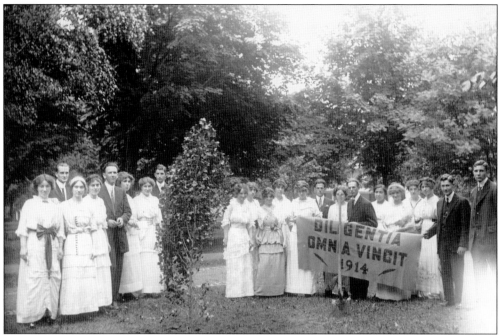

The class has just planted a tree to commemorate their time at the Genesee Wesleyan Seminary. Their banner proclaims that they will be persistent and diligent in all worthy endeavors.

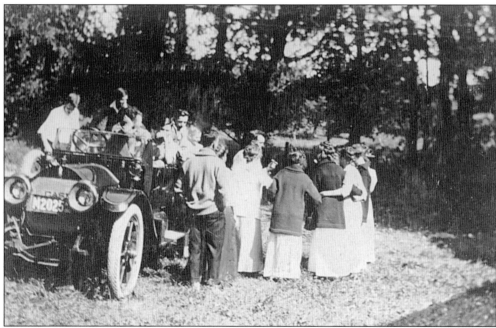

The Day We Got Our Start is more about sad endings as the class embraces one last time. With the allied powers deep in a vicious war, the future looks bleak as it is now certain the United States cannot remain neutral. Outings to the lakes are less frequent and made with fewer friends as college and war enlistment plans are made.

Four

CORNELL, CHIMEMASTERS, AND MUD RUSHES

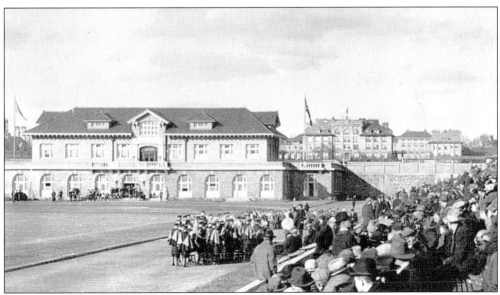

A band salutes graduates on the playing field of Schoellkopf Memorial Stadium. To the right, in the distance, are the majestic buildings of the College of Agriculture. The architectural grandeur of Cornell certainly rivaled anything in Europe. George Corby attended the university from 1917 to 1920 and would even teach photography while there.

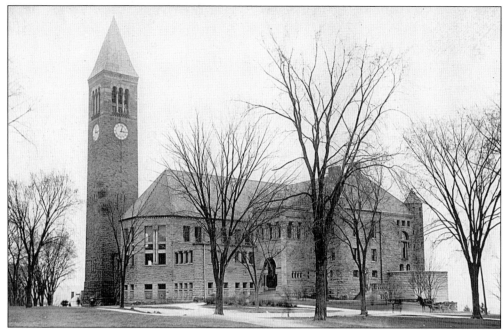

Local architect William Henry Miller designed the 173-foot McGraw Tower and the adjacent Uris Library. The tower holds the renowned Cornell chimes, which have since been recast and expanded from 9 to 21 bells. Chimemasters still compete for the honor of climbing the 161 steps to play concerts. The tower also holds an 1875 Seth Thomas clock with a 14-foot pendulum.

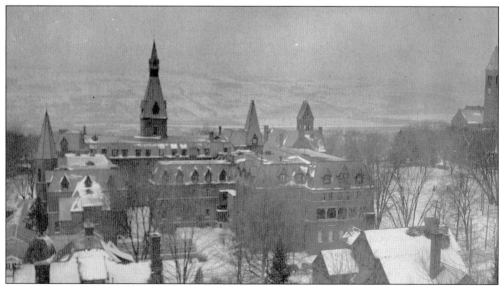

A winter's view looks past the spires and frosty gables of Sage Hall to the shores rising from Cayuga Lake. Henry William Sage established Sage College with the intent that women would have equal access to education at Cornell. The structure was considered Cornell's architectural masterpiece when it opened in 1875.

84

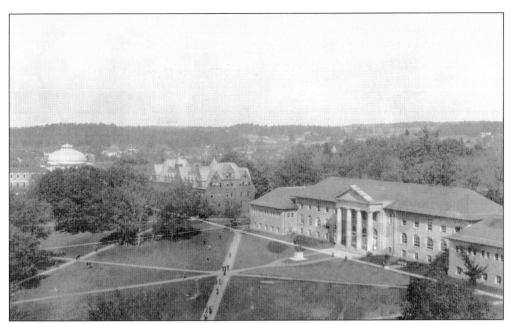
A look from McGraw Tower toward the Arts Quad shows Goldwin Smith Hall.

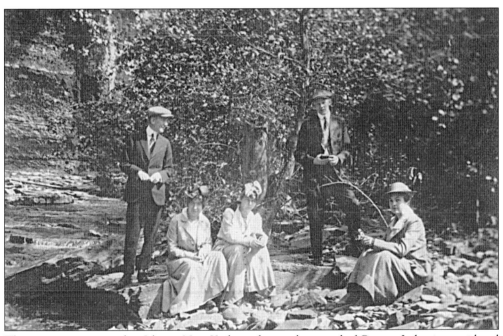
The university, situated in Ithaca, New York, at the southern end of Cayuga Lake, is considered one of the most beautiful campuses in the world. It was built on a hilltop fret with gorges, cascades, waterfalls, and spectacular views. Here George Corby and fellow students enjoy a hike along one of the scenic waterways. Equally impressive is nearby Ithaca College.

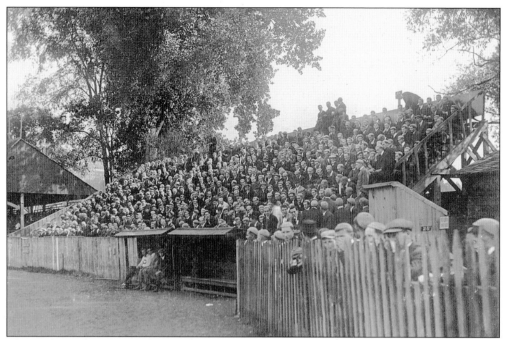

The steel stand is full as Cornell's and Colgate's football teams go at it.

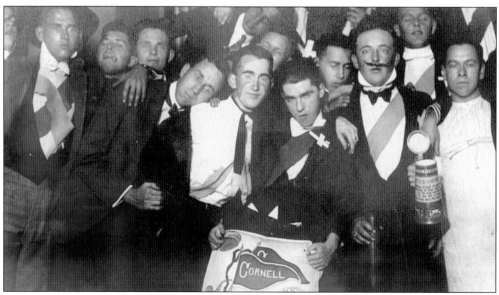

George Corby and his Kappa Delta Rho brothers mug for the camera during a "farce" where beer obviously flowed freely. The fraternity was dedicated to the ideals of "truth, justice and virtue."

A campus dandy, barely tolerable to his more subdued friend, obviously came from a well-off family. He looks like he stepped off the fashion pages of Collier's. Impeccable in a tailored quality serge jacket and cotton pants, his four-in-hand silk tie is perfectly tied and his pocket kerchief neatly folded. The shirt has detachable collar and cuffs that could be separately starched and ironed. He holds behind him an ultra-fashionable fedora hat with a white band.

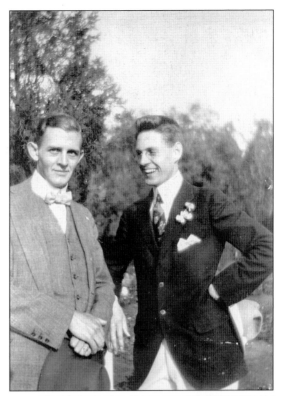

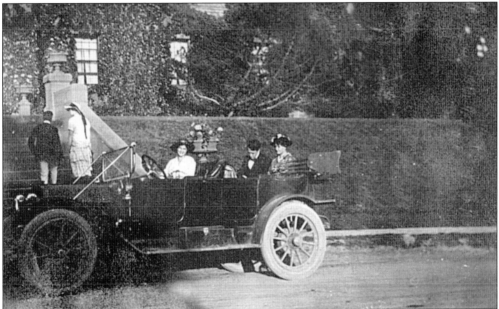

In this photograph titled *Those Goodbye Girls*, a story is told. Two couples have returned after a day of touring. Tired chaperones are in the back seat as one couple bids good night on the steps of Sage Hall. George Corby was influenced by magazine illustrators of the day, among them Norman Rockwell, who told stories with their paintings. George often composed his photographs with a story in mind.

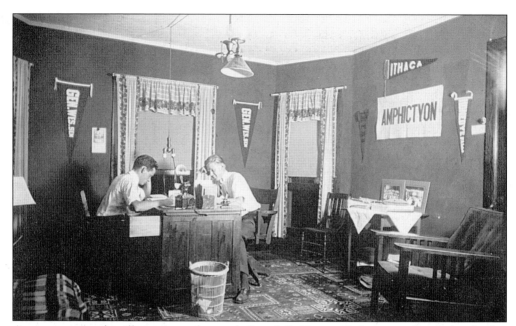

A roommate ponders illustrations of young ladies while George Corby pretends to be hard at his books in their dormitory. Telling a story is again the purpose of the photograph. Corby was an avid magazine reader and was impressed by the artist illustrators of the day who told stories with their renderings. *Boy's Life* magazine had as its primary illustrator Norman Rockwell, who at age 19 was only a year older than Corby.

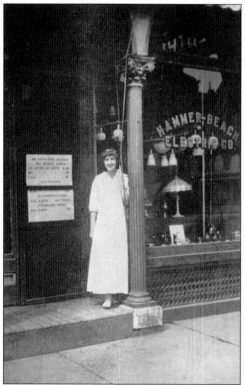

While on a visit to a lake country city, this young lady was photographed in the entrance of Hammer-Beach Electric Company. During processing of the image, highlights were added to the column and step for drama.

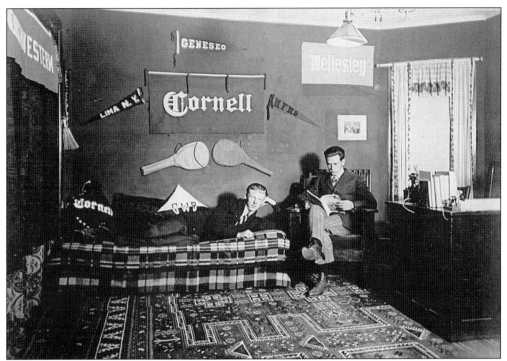

The walls of the sleeping apartment bear pennants from Lima, Geneseo, Honeoye Falls High School, and Genesee Wesleyan Seminary.

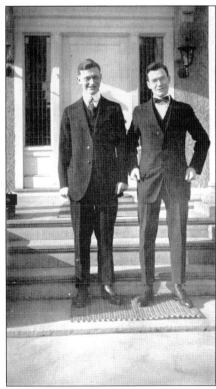

These eager chaps are Kappa Delta Rho brothers. The fraternity was founded at Cornell.

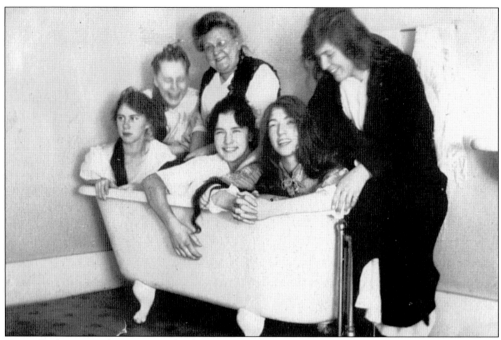

Even the housemother—center back—is getting into the fun as George Corby coaxes all of them into a claw-foot bathtub at a Sage dormitory.

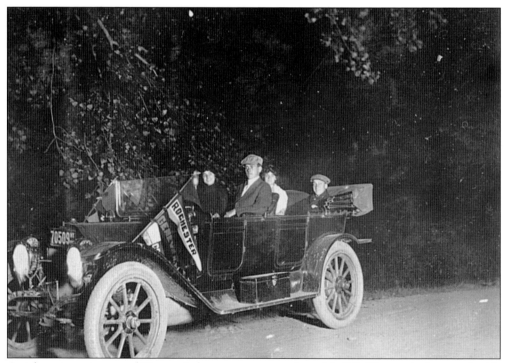

A sightseeing trip around Cayuga Lake comes to an end at nightfall. The car is decorated with Rochester and Genesee College pennants.

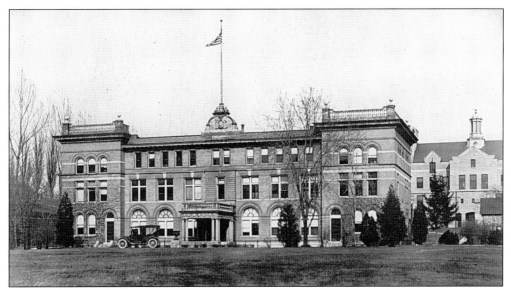

James Law Hall opened in 1894 as a home for Cornell's veterinary studies. James Law was the college's first professor of veterinary medicine. The elegant yellow brick structure was razed 65 years later to make way for the School of Industrial and Labor Relations. The veterinary school was relocated to updated facilities.

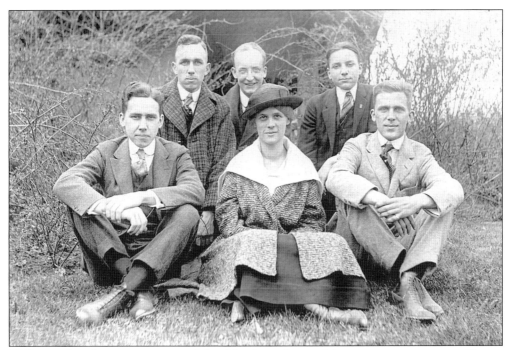

Well-attired students pose on a cool day. Members of one of the campus organizations George Corby belonged to, they appear savvy and politically astute. Beyond that, they were not adverse to pranks, lampooning, and other campus shenanigans.

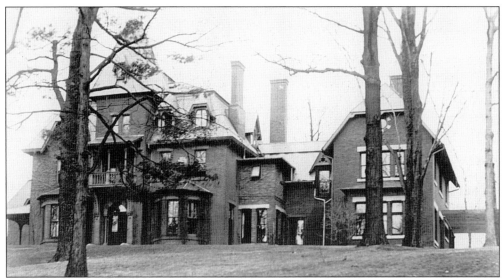

Andrew Dickson White's residence was built in 1871 in the High-Victorian Gothic style. White was the cofounder and first president of the university. Below is a view of one of the front rooms.

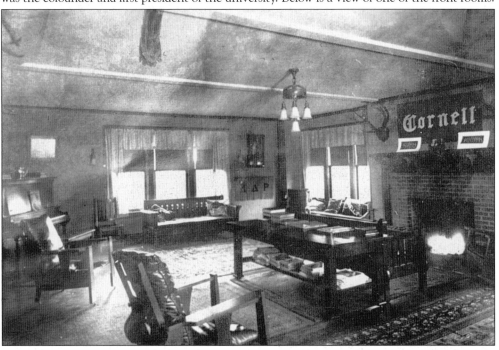

Jennie McGraw had this mansion built in 1880 on a site just below the present Johnson Art Museum. She was in Europe during construction and married Cornell's first librarian while in Rome. She died a month after returning to the states, having never enjoyed her magnificent new home. The Chi Psi fraternity purchased it in the mid-1890s. In 1906, it was destroyed by fire with the loss of four students and three firemen. The photographer of this stereo view is not known.

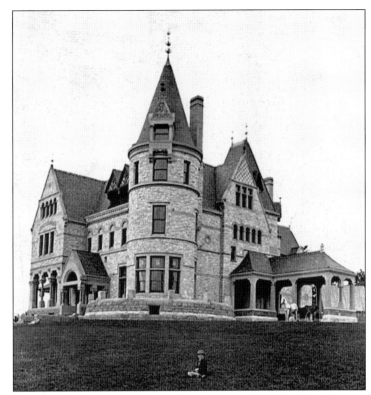

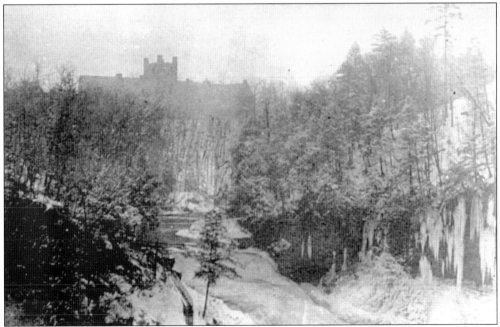

The battlement-style tower of Prudence Risley Hall looms in a kind of medieval gloom over the wintry depths of Fall Creek gorge. The hall opened in 1912 and was used as an additional women's dormitory. The desire to make the campus resemble those in Europe was achieved with this structure. The interior even features a grand English Tudor dining room.

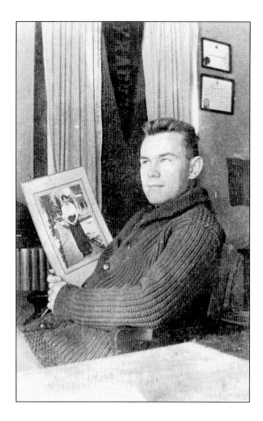

A fellow wearing a cardigan sweater keeps warm in his chilly dormitory with longing thoughts of his girlfriend.

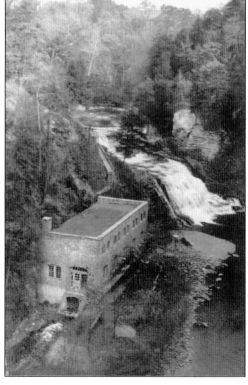

This little hydroelectric power plant, photographed from the suspension bridge across Fall Creek, was built in 1904. A raceway diverted water from the falls, which spun a turbine. Fall Creek, as early as 1818, powered a small industrial hub that included sawmills, paper mills, gristmills, and plaster mills. Much of it was transported on Cayuga Lake steamers starting in the 1820s.

Sporting knickerbocker pants (knickers) and a three-piece serge suit, George Corby is roughish in this self-portrait. The overcoat is a tan linen duster with sleeve tabs, used often when driving. His shoes, canvas Oxfords, are mud-caked, suggesting he has been hiking along the campus gorges taking pictures. While at Cornell, he was a member of the Arts Cross Country Team, the University Rifle Team, Cornell Masonic Club, and Cornell's Officer's Club.

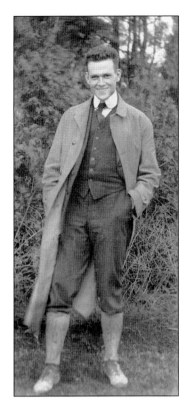

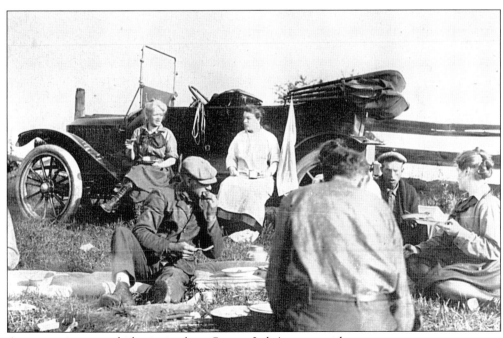

A group enjoys a roadside picnic along Cayuga Lake's countryside.

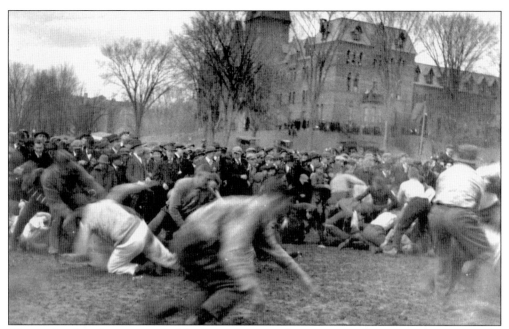

The mud rush, a hazing ritual of freshmen by upperclassmen, is underway on the quadrangle. Below, in a photograph titled *After the Underclass Rush*, George Corby and his pals proudly display the results of their mud-spattering brawl.

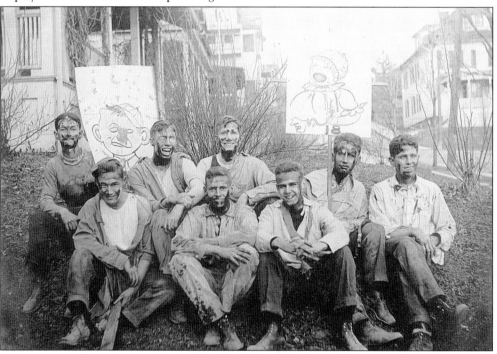

Appearing slightly dazed but proud nonetheless, another survivor of the mud rush has his picture taken.

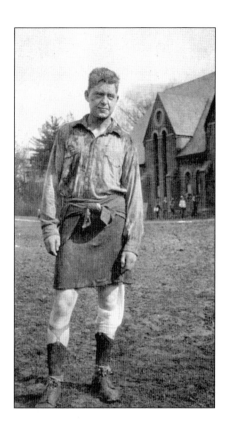

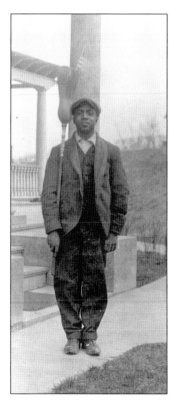

A campus employee strikes a military pose. Clearly the war was preeminent in the thoughts of many.

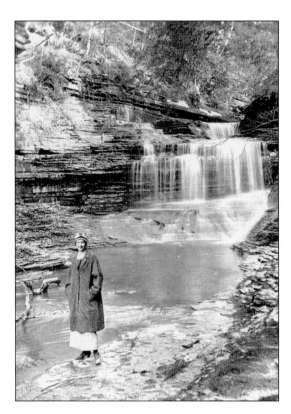

The region around Ithaca is famous for beautiful waterfalls. Student Evelyn "Slim" Hieber is photographed with one of the falls in the Buttermilk chain in the distance. Buttermilk, Enfield, and Taughannock Falls would become state parks in the mid-1920s.

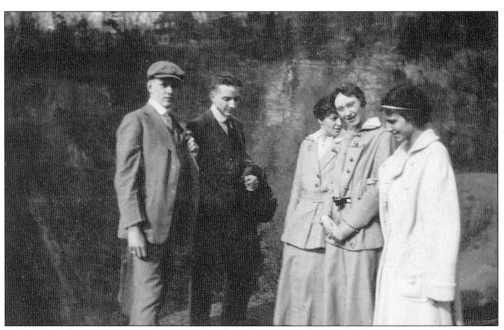

After breakfast, it is time for a weekend exploration of one of the gorges situated within the campus.

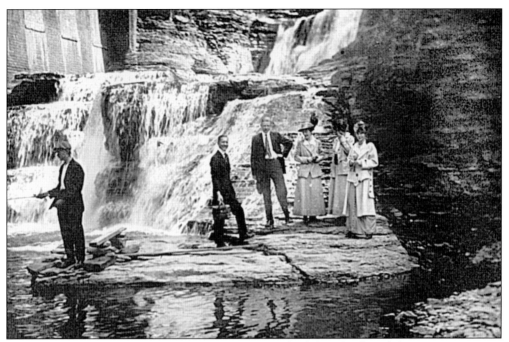

Triphammer Falls on the campus provides a stunning backdrop for these hikers.

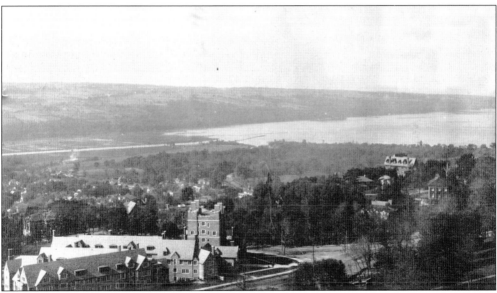

In this view from the campus toward Ithaca and the southern end of the lake it is easy to see how Cornell's alma mater was inspired; "Far above Cayuga's waters." The rolling hills, part of the original Phelps Gorham Purchase, contain Amish and Mennonite settlements. It was known as the Burned-Over District where a second revival of Christianity occurred in the 19th century. Most of the lakes are deep, creating unique microclimates. A lake-effect warmness keeps the vineyards from freezing.

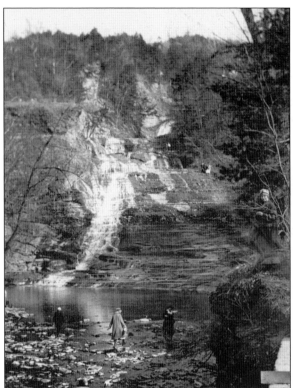

Hikers explore along the pool at the foot of Buttermilk Falls. Located two miles south of Ithaca, Buttermilk Creek makes a 500-foot drop through hanging gorges. The rigorous hike along the creek is rewarded with stunning views of waterfalls, cascades, rapids, and steep canyons.

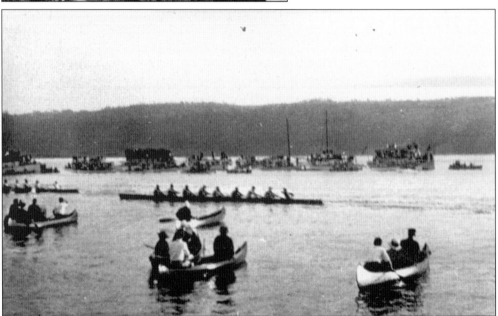

Cornell freshmen are defeating Harvard in the Spring Day varsity races along the east shore of the lake. Most photographs are dim because the races were held later in the day when lake winds died down. In the distance are spectator and judge boats. Lehigh Valley Railroad brought hundreds to the Ivy-League event on their Auburn branch. Spectators could watch from gondola cars fitted with special bleachers.

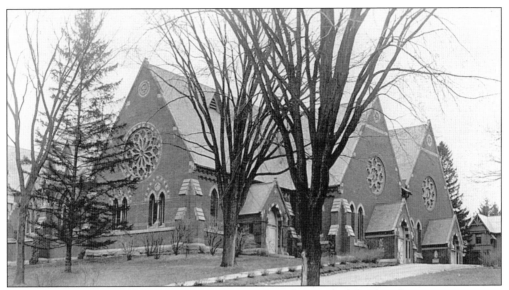

Andrew Dickson White and Ezra Cornell were bitterly attacked for founding a nonsectarian university. Both were religious but wanted Cornell to be free of any religious domination. However, worship was certainly encouraged, and Sage Chapel was provided in 1875. It is home to the oldest student group, the Cornell Glee Club. It also boasted the first outdoor electric lighting system installed in the belfry in 1879.

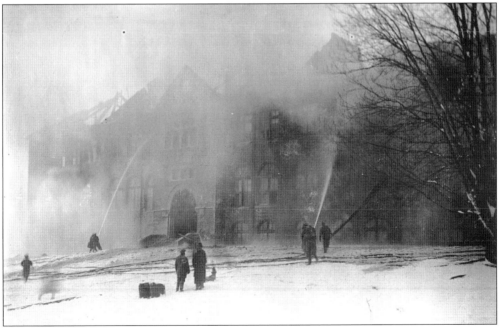

The university's chemistry department, Morse Hall, was destroyed by fire in February 1916. It was named in honor of Samuel F. B. Morse, inventor of the telegraph. Sixty years earlier, Ezra Cornell stood at this location and envisioned his university. The Johnson Museum of Art now occupies this site.

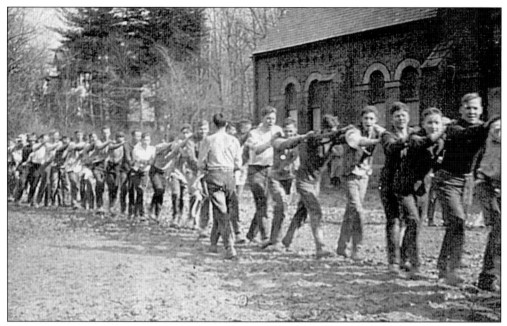

The caterpillar, a campus tradition, is underway. The long line would weave its way around the campus.

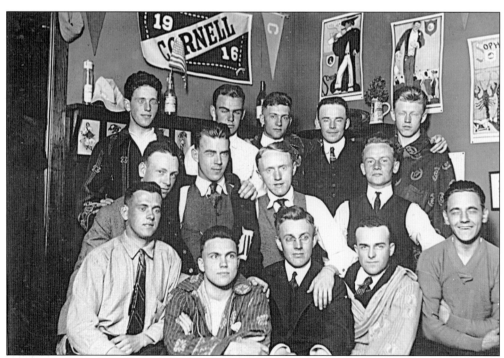

Brothers of the Beta Chapter of Kappa Delta Rho pose in a photograph titled *Aunt Maggie Sullivan's Boys*. The fraternity had over 75 chapters nationwide.

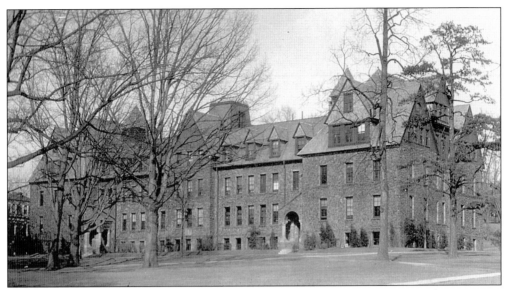

Andrew Dickson White was less than pleased when Lincoln Hall, the home for civil engineering and architecture, was designed as a brick structure. Insisting that it be built of stone to match other buildings on the Arts Quad, an additional $7,000 was appropriated—enough for a stone facade and sides. The back is built of brick.

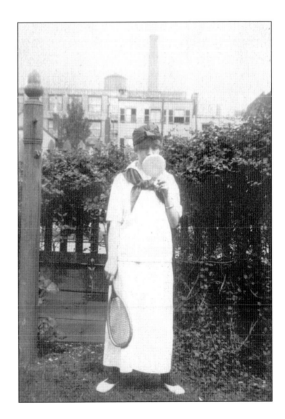

A student peeks forlornly in a mirror after a tennis game.

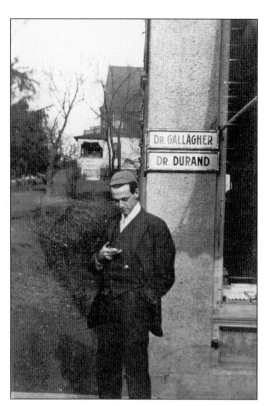

In *Waiting for a Car*, George Corby wonders where the trolley is to take him from Ithaca back up to the campus. Trolley cars made the rugged ascent to the college, passing Cascadilla Hall on a private right-of-way.

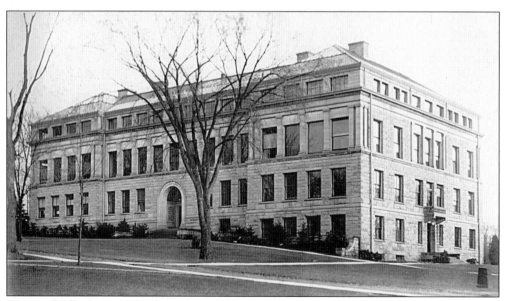

Stimson Hall, the university's medical college, was built in 1902. It was named for Lewis A. Stimson, a famous surgeon and one of the school's original professors.

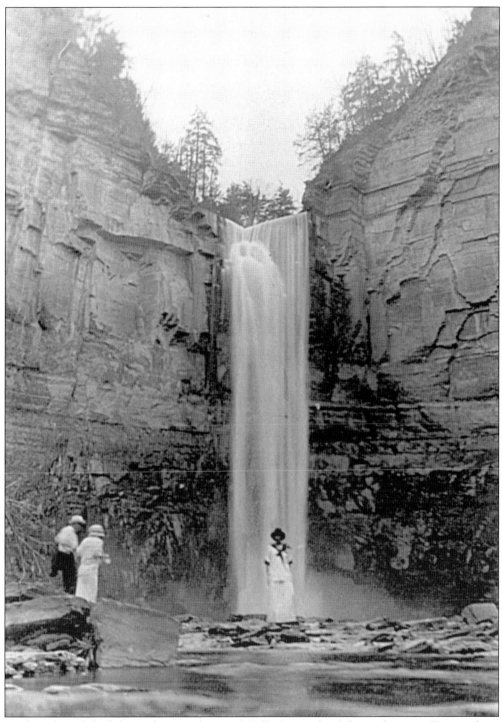

Students have hiked the trail to Taughannock Falls. Located in Ulysses, between Trumansburg and Ithaca, the incredible 215-foot falls is one of the highest east of the Rocky Mountains. It is one of many glens and gorges whose waterways have cut through the countryside to reach one of the Finger Lakes.

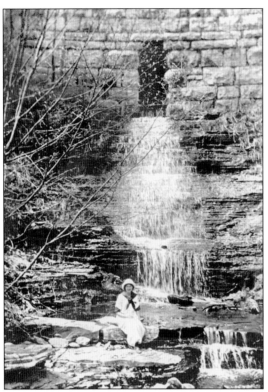

A sluiceway was designed into the stone Lehigh Valley Railroad bridge to allow a watercourse to flow somewhat uninterrupted. Friend Elaine is sitting at the foot of the falls. Wonderful settings like this continue to draw students from schools in the Finger Lake region.

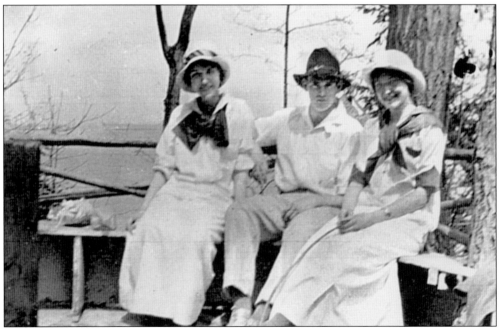

Relaxing in a pavilion along the trail, George Corby and two friends smile for the camera. Of course only proper summer attire was worn. The girls are wearing loose-fitting poplin middy coats. They tended to be white with green, blue, or rose collars and trim. Corby is wearing an Alpine hat and men's outing shirt with a convertible sport collar.

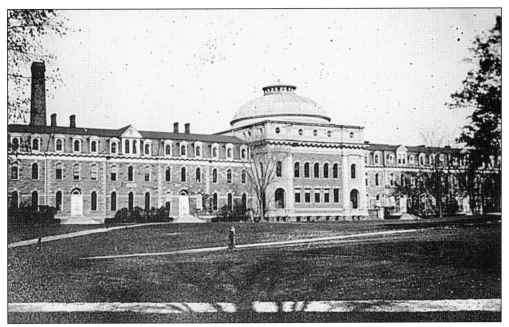

Original funding for Sibley Hall came from telegraph magnate and charter trustee Hiram Sibley of Rochester. Constructed in 1870 as a home for mechanical engineering, it was gradually enlarged by Sibley's son Hiram W. Sibley.

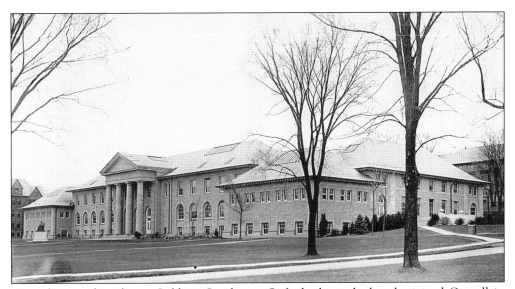

A much-revered professor, Goldwin Smith was Oxford educated when he joined Cornell in its early days. In 1906, Goldwin Smith Hall was dedicated in his honor. It houses academic departments such as classics and philosophy and the administrative offices of the College of Arts and Sciences.

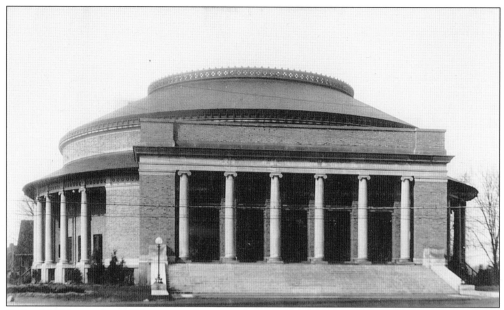

Bailey Hall opened in 1913 as an auditorium. It was named after Liberty Hall Bailey, a professor and administrator influential in the establishment of the College of Agriculture. Here Cornellians enjoyed first-rate orchestras and art exhibits from around the world. The colonnaded auditorium housed one of the 8,000 pipe organs Dale Carnegie gave to concert halls and churches between 1874 and 1919.

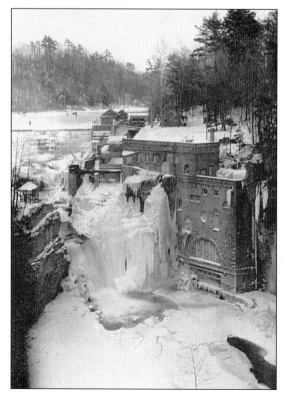

The Hydraulic Lab, located in Fall Gorge and powered by Triphammer Falls, is encrusted with thick ice. The 1902 lab was used for studies in hydraulics and power generation through turbines. The lab was powered from water diverted along a canal off Beebe Lake (upper left). The lake was also used for university hockey games.

Ezra Cornell would die before his palatial residence Llenroc (Cornell spelled in reverse) was completed. Cornell made his fortune in the telegraph business through association with Samuel Morse. In 1865, he cofounded Cornell University with Andrew Dickson White. The residence remained in the family for several decades before being acquired by the local Delta Phi fraternity. The photographer is unknown.

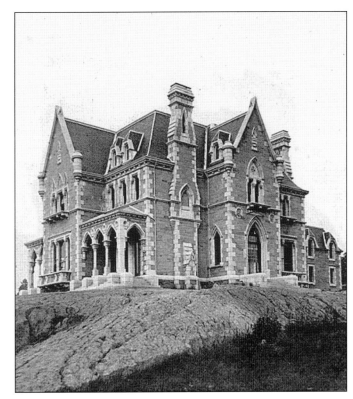

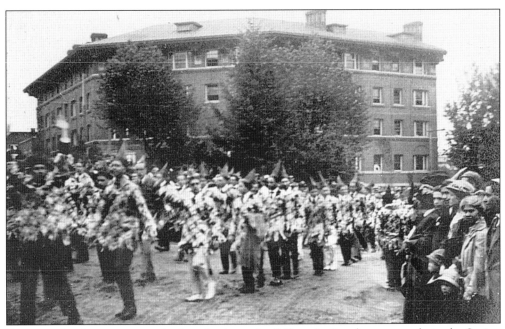

Fraternity brothers, wearing checkered suits and tall "beanies," make a spectacle in the Spring Day parade. The daylong celebration took place in town as well as on campus. The location is Sheldon Court in college town. The Triangle Bookstore later became a residence hall.

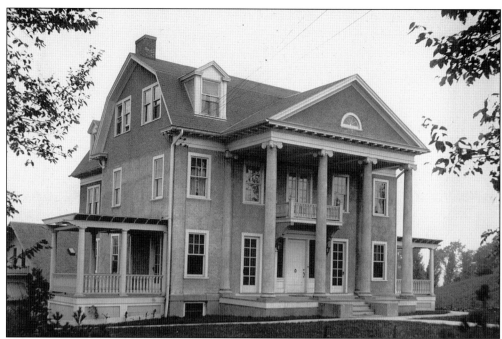

This substantial structure was the first home of Kappa Delta Rho, founded in 1913. In addition to breakfasts, dinners, fund-raisers, and recitals, general get-togethers took place where students and professors mingled and discussed campus and world affairs. The emergence of destructive philosophies such as communism and fascism would certainly have been discussed. The woman below, sitting on one of the flanking porches, has the inquisitive gaze of a teacher interested in a student's insights.

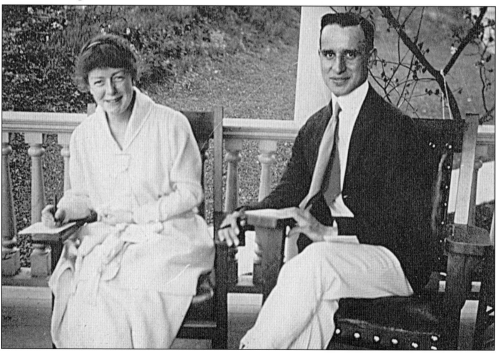

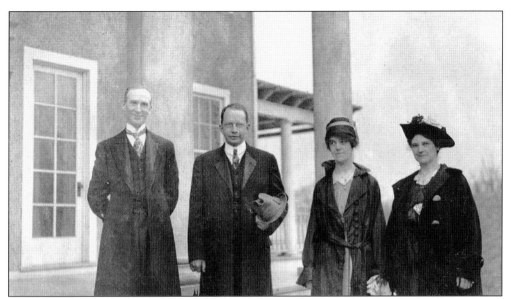

Administrators and guests attend functions at the Kappa Delta Rho home at 306 Highland Avenue.

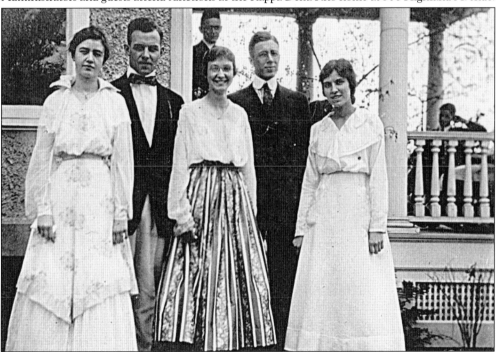

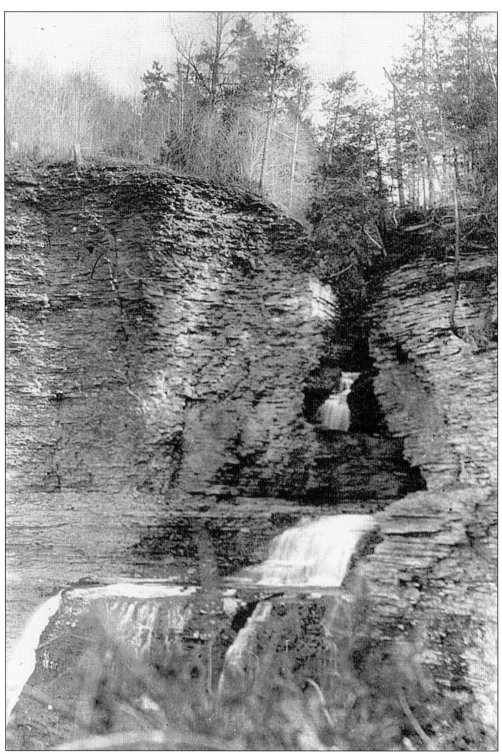

One of the falls in the Buttermilk chain descends its rocky steps. This shows the tenacity of narrow watercourses to cut their way down through hundreds of feet of rock to reach the lakes.

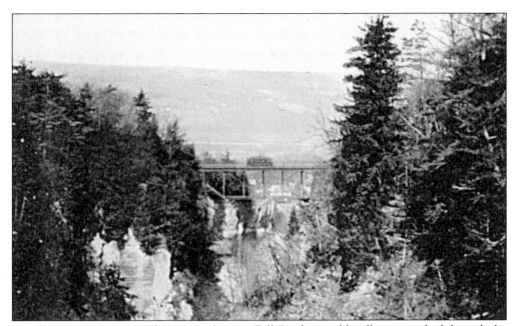

A trolley crosses the Steward Street Bridge over Fall Creek. An old trolley was pushed through the guard railing and into the gorge during the filming of a movie. Ithaca, because of its many gorges, was a major center for filming action-packed cliffhangers during the silent film era (1910–1920). The rugged countryside was used in such serials as the *Perils of Pauline*. Wharton Brothers Studio in Ithaca produced many such films.

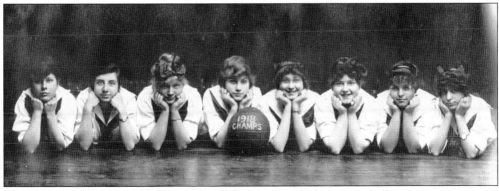

Cornell's women's basketball champions of 1918 pose with their game ball.

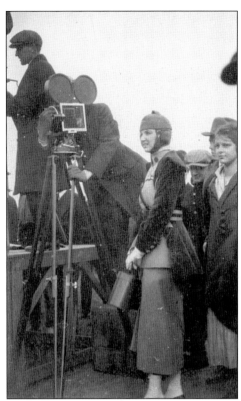

Women in costume wait while a scene is set up during filming of a wartime film on the Cornell campus. Below, movie cameras are made ready and the script is checked. Cayuga Lake is visible in the background.

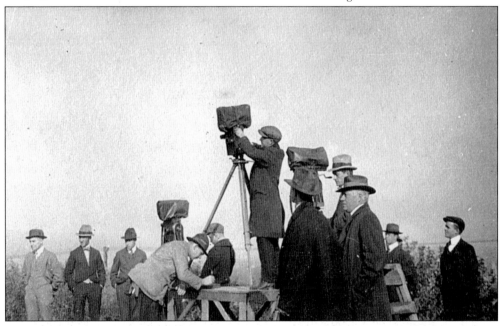

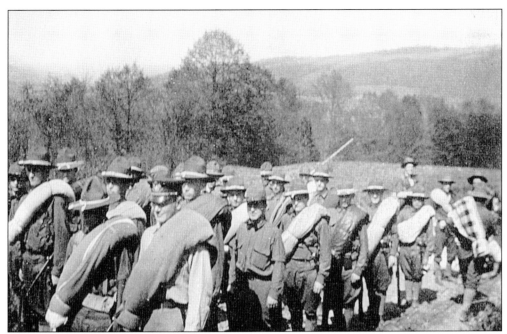

George Corby interrupted college to serve with the National Guard during the Mexican border incident in 1916 under General Pershing. He then enlisted the day the United States entered World War I. Cornell had an aggressive recruitment program. This brigade of Army ROTC cadets is marching from the campus to Newfield, a town in Tompkins County near Ithaca.

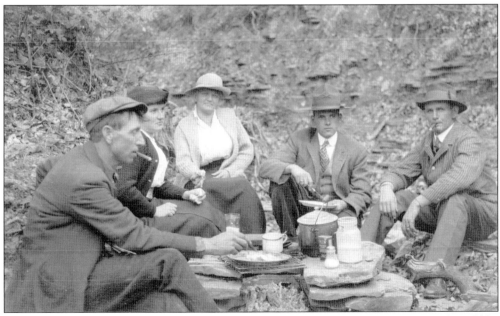

A roadside picnic near Ithaca was photographed by George's brother Bruce Corby and would be manufactured as a postcard.

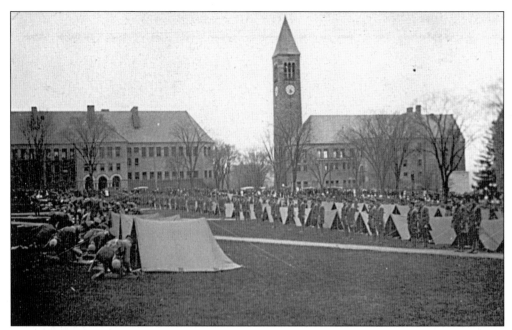

A sea of tents fills the Arts Quad as Cornell's Army ROTC puts on an impressive display of their war readiness. A form of the program dates back to 1862 and was reestablished by the National Defense Act of 1916. The purpose was to recruit and educate commissioned officers, since West Point could not produce enough on its own.

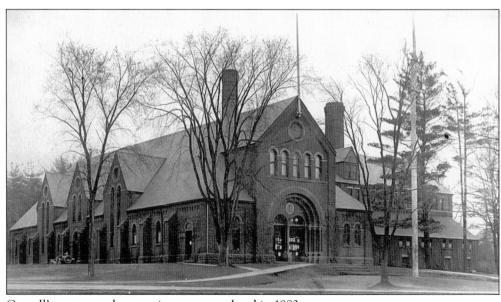

Cornell's armory and gymnasium was completed in 1883.

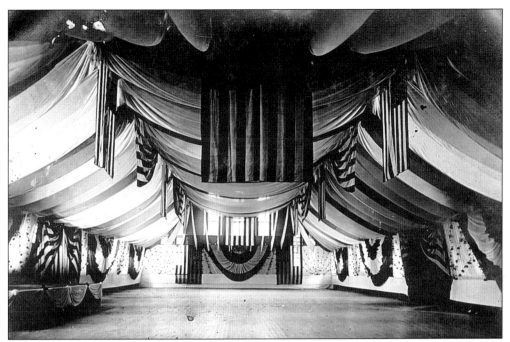

The armory is boldly regaled in sails of patriotic bunting as a combination dance and rally, called a military hop, is prepared.

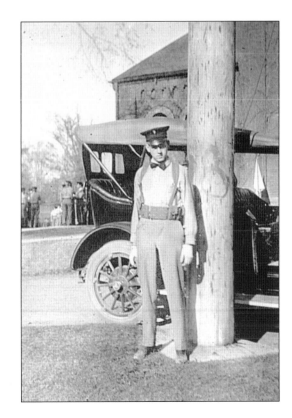

A recruit stands near the armory during bugle call.

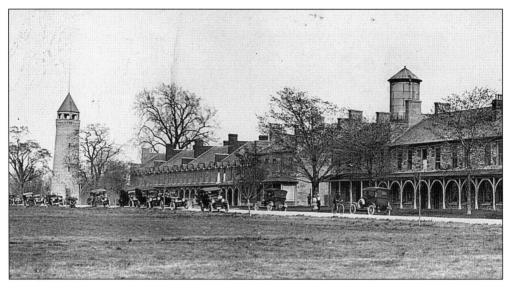

George Corby was stationed for a while at Madison Barracks in Sackets Harbor, New York. The "Old Stone Row" dates back to 1819. The Romanesque Revival stone tower was built 1892 as part of a new water system. The unique complex of stone buildings is now a museum of military architecture.

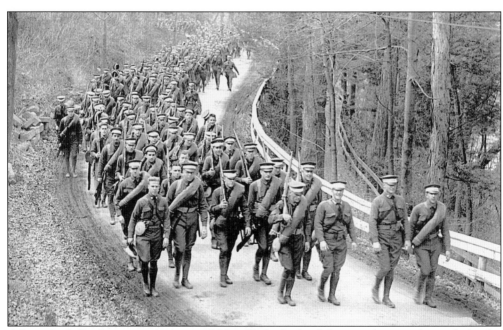

A brigade drills along a road in central New York. Corby did some photography work for the military during his enlistment.

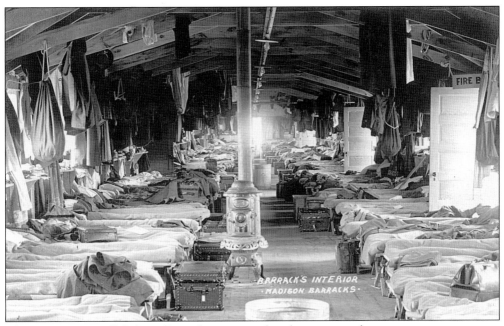

This interior view of Madison Barracks was reproduced as a postcard.

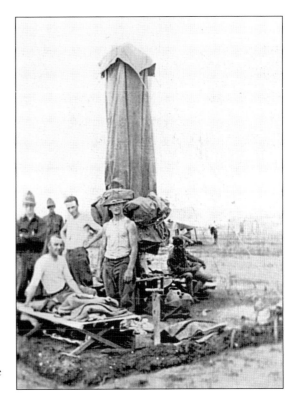

Army life meant hours of boredom for enlisted men, but Corby did not have to look far to find interesting subjects. Here a detachment practices decamping.

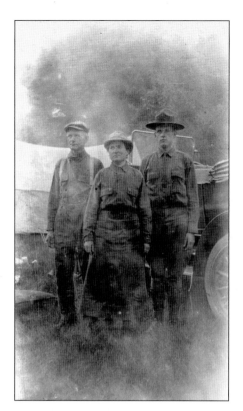

Campfire smoke and morning mist drift through a campsite outside the Madison Barracks as Oscar and Estella Corby visit their son George (right). George made sure to get the old touring car and tent in his patriotic composition.

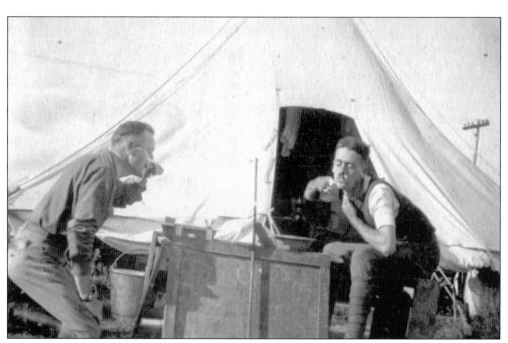

Two soldiers take their morning shaves seriously, creating an expressive photograph of otherwise mundane camp life.

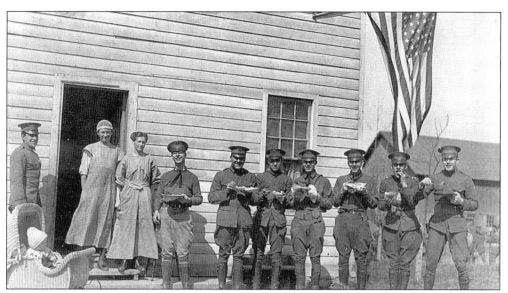

Soldiers are delighted with what these proud women have whipped up for lunch at the mess hall.

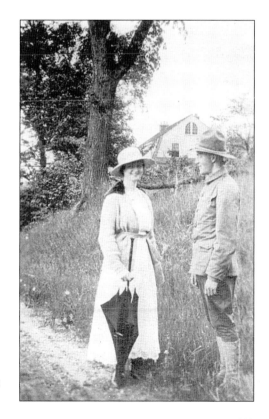

A young lady and soldier converse on a country lane near the barracks. No matter what turmoil human existence brings, there is always time for love.

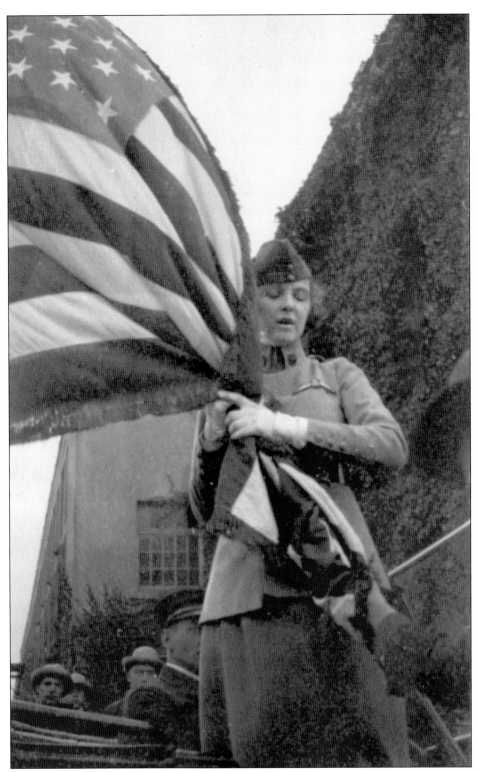

A patriot clutches a flag during a celebration on the Cornell campus.

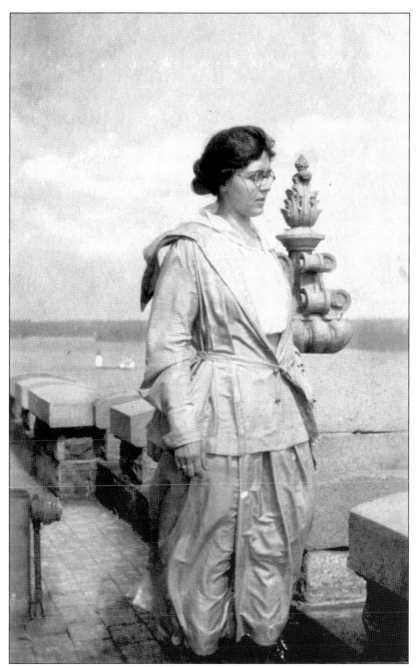

While on leave, George Corby posed this friend on the battlements of Bolt Castle in New York's 1,000 Islands. George C. Bolt, millionaire proprietor of the Waldorf Astoria, began the castle. When his wife died suddenly in 1904, Bolt, brokenhearted, ordered all work on the castle to cease. Workers left tools, nails, and crated treasures where they lay. This woman stands fixed, almost sculpturally, atop the castle. Her expression is mixed. Women have just won the right to vote, but the world is still in mourning for the millions killed in the war. It seems that humanity could at least breathe again. It could take in air like that blowing over these battlements—battlements built to project sentiments of love.

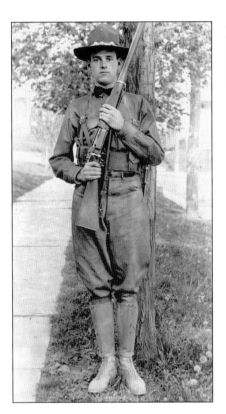

During his 25 years of service, George Corby would become a second lieutenant in the infantry of the reserve corp; first lieutenant in infantry of the national army; and finally a major in the reserves.

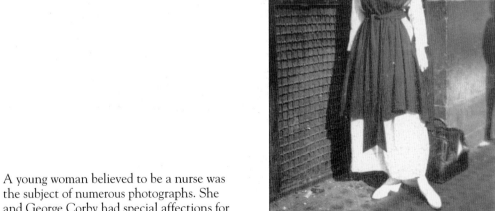

A young woman believed to be a nurse was the subject of numerous photographs. She and George Corby had special affections for each other.

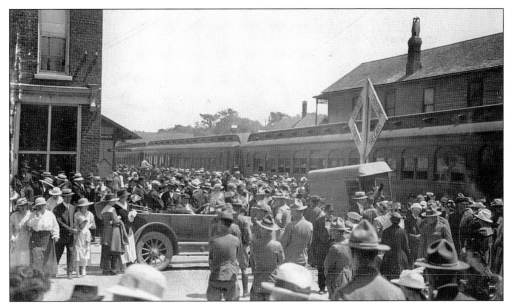

The New York Central depot at Sackets Harbor is congested with family and friends as transports bring the doughboys home. There is a horse-drawn ambulance right of center.

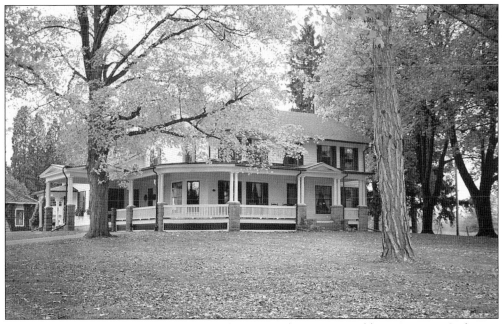

The Lima home is seen here as it looks today, having been preserved by great-niece Catharine Corby Gardner and her husband, Marty Gardner. The home has appeared in newspaper articles and on national television.

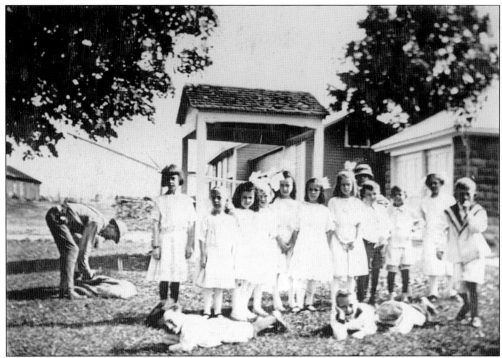

Children attending Bruce Corby's birthday party around 1913 are about to enjoy homemade ice cream that has been kept cool down in the well. Below is the well house, as it appears today, and the pump still works! Many of the outbuildings remain, including an outhouse with plastered walls. The two silos are all that are left of the primary dairy barn, which burned in 1971, effectively ending the Corbys' dairy business.

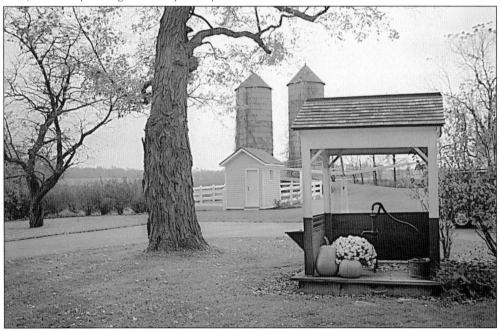

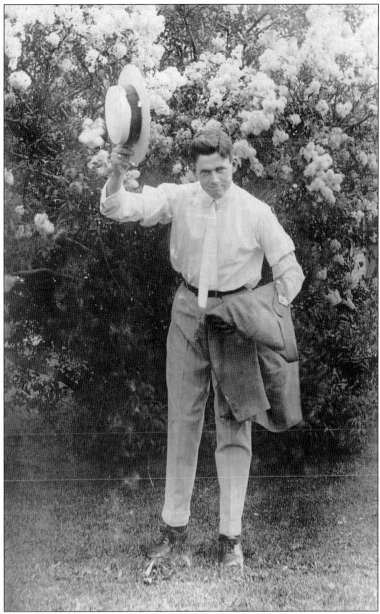

With a courteous tip of the hat, George Corby bids adieu, with imagined hopes that his photographic legacy was enjoyed. Sophisticated, good-humored, and never far from pretty ladies, he was a master photographer whose photographs brought much entertainment to Lima and Honeoye Falls. His close-ups of Queen Elizabeth and her sister Princes Margaret, taken at their winter retreat, were particularly impressive. But farming was his life, and he never fully recovered from the loss of his dairy business to fire in 1971. He and his wife, Irene, traveled extensively, especially to Barbados. Irene was at his side when he died in 1977 at age 82. Closing his albums seems to lock him and his friends in an eternal rhythm where they are forever young to enjoy endless summers in the lake country. The clatter of the Lehigh Valley milk train and the call of "Its haying time!" never cease. It looks like they were just regular folk who lived fairly ordinary lives. Corby, through his lens, wanted people to know they were good lives.

ACROSS AMERICA, PEOPLE ARE DISCOVERING SOMETHING WONDERFUL. *THEIR HERITAGE.*

Arcadia Publishing is the leading local history publisher in the United States. With more than 3,000 titles in print and hundreds of new titles released every year, Arcadia has extensive specialized experience chronicling the history of communities and celebrating America's hidden stories, bringing to life the people, places, and events from the past. To discover the history of other communities across the nation, please visit:

www.arcadiapublishing.com

Customized search tools allow you to find regional history books about the town where you grew up, the cities where your friends and family live, the town where your parents met, or even that retirement spot you've been dreaming about.

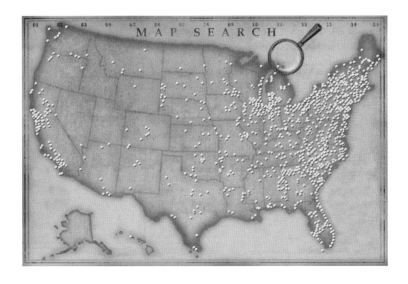